The
GLORY
of
HIS RISING

The
GLORY
of
HIS RISING

Volume Two of the TRIUMPH TRILOGY

Neil M. Fraser

GOSPEL FOLIO PRESS
304 Killaly St. West, Port Colborne, ON L3K 6A6
Available in the UK from
JOHN RITCHIE LTD., Kilmarnock, Scotland

THE GLORY OF HIS RISING
by Neil M Fraser
Copyright © 2001
Gospel Folio Press
All rights reserved

Previously published by Loizeaux Brothers, Inc., Neptune, NJ, 1963

Published by Gospel Folio Press
304 Killaly St. W.
Port Colborne, ON L3K 6A6

ISBN 1-882701-67-4

Cover design by J. B. Nicholson, Jr.

All Scripture quotations from the King James Version unless
otherwise noted.

Printed in the United States of America

Author's Foreword

One cannot write on the *Grandeur of Golgotha* without desiring to attempt a companion book on the glory of our Lord's rising from the dead. One feels that if he has spoken of Him who was delivered for our offenses, he must equally speak of Him who was raised again for our justification. It is not so much that he would examine the roots of his faith; it is rather that he would share with others the fruits of it.

The resurrection is not only the proof of a work perfectly accomplished on the cross; it is the pledge of a work to be done in all who have believed its message. *"For if we have been planted in the likeness of His death, we shall be also in the likeness of His resurrection"* (Rom. 6:5).

NEIL M. FRASER
Eugene, Oregon

Introduction

In these pages we do not attempt to furnish much in the way of philosophical proof of the resurrection of Jesus. To us it is not a thing incredible that God should raise *Him* from the dead; it would be rather incredible if He were *not* raised. The common human experience of non-resurrection is reversed in the case of Jesus Christ.

The Gospel records which give us the story of Christ are self-authenticating. They bear the marks of credibility. If they are fabrications they must have been formed independently or in collusion. But the agreements are too numerous for the former, and the apparent discrepancies for the latter. The documents have been examined as no other ancient writings have been by legal minds whose training has enabled them to apply methods known to them for discovering the truth or falsity of evidence. They have pronounced them genuine.

While apologetics are useful in confirming faith, they do not, as a rule, create it. True faith does not stand in the wisdom of men. We believe there is an artlessness about the story of Jesus Christ that is both convincing and conclusive. When we have read the earlier part of His life where His flawless character is not categorically stated but portrayed, we feel that His rising again from the dead is natural and proper. It is the ultimate vindication of His claims, the logical sequence to His death.

The Gospel writers never seek to praise Jesus, or point out His virtues. They are not trying to create an atmosphere conducive to faith. They do not seem to care whether you believe or not (if we exclude John), since they boldly declare things which had better been left out, if they were writing for effect. They are writing about a life perfectly natural, yet evidently naturally perfect.

When you read the account of our Lord's rising from the dead, you feel that His proven veracity in other matters is once more demonstrated in the fulfillment of His own prediction that He would rise again. As the virgin birth stands at the beginning of that perfect life on earth as the producing cause, so the resurrection stands at the end as the natural consequence of that life laid down. It was not fitting that the corn of wheat, in dying, should abide alone (see Jn. 12:24).

Neither is it our purpose to attempt a harmony of the accounts of His rising in the four Gospels. Where others might see human contradiction, we only see evidence of the selection and superintendency of the divine Spirit. Each writer takes only that which is relevant to his subject, as we shall see, and the omissions are as significant as the admissions. If Matthew the Jew says nothing of the principal appearances of Christ in Jerusalem, and Luke the Gentile nothing of the Galilean appearances, to us this is deeply significant and demands closer scrutiny. All four writers—alike noting the witness of the women, yet differing in its collective and individual character— give us a manifestation of design and purpose. There is a designed difference between the accounts of the disciple-evangelists Matthew and John, and those of Mark and Luke.

These who write concerning His rising are not presenting carefully compared and cold facts, but giving experiences as they were wrought in the hearts and minds of men and women. Subjective experiences are prominent amid the objective facts of the narratives.

Then, too, as angelic appearance was active at our Lord's birth, so we may be sure that the angelic world was much more moved at this "second birth" of the Saviour. This explains the seeming contradictory accounts of angels at His resurrection. As John Peter Lange observed, the Easter message is not a solo, nor is it heard in the simple and beautiful melody of a chorus, but in the higher music of a *fugue* where the apparent conflict of the individual voices are observed to blend into a harmonious and balanced whole. We take these accounts as they stand.

The conduct of the disciples of the Lord after His rising precludes any idea of fraud or hallucination. The witnesses are too many and their witness too costly. More than five hundred seeing Him at one time must preclude hallucination. They had the evidence of their senses. Rogues under the pressure and pain of persecution would soon have confessed fraud. These disciples died for their faith. After their first shock of surprise and fear—for they did not anticipate His death, much less His rising again—they never doubted the evidence. Only a triumphant Christ could have made them triumphant.

A leader who did not actually die, but survived the ordeal of crucifixion, could never have inspired His followers to believe that He was a conqueror over death and then sent them forth to face a hostile world. His emaciated appearance could only have aroused their pity and given the lie to His claims. But inspire them He did, enabling them to preach a message which in turn aroused the fiercest antagonism of Jew and Gentile alike. The resurrection story was not a "benevolent conspiracy" by men who thought the end justified the means.

It is noteworthy that the Jews did not seek to crush the movement of Christianity by evidence of such fraud, but by threats and persecution. The failure on their part to produce the body of Jesus, and thus to put an end to the preaching of the disciples, is as weighty as would be the phenomenon of these disciples suffering and dying to propagate faith in a leader's resurrection if his decaying body had been in their possession. Their martyrdom was the costly evidence of their faith.

As they had plenty of evidence for the reality of His death, and ratified it by His burial, so did they have for

His identity in resurrection. It was this same Jesus, yet with none of the imposed limitations of His tabernacle of flesh before His death. Like the bodies of His own who live by Him, which, sown in natural bodies are raised in spiritual ones, our Lord in resurrection has a body with new powers, enabling Him to leave the grave clothes undisturbed in the tomb, and later to enter the upper room, the doors being shut.

Our purpose is instead to glory in the fact of His rising and to grasp the significance of it insofar as we are able. Paul sees in it a proof of His deity in Romans 1:4, a passage which evidently includes the resurrection of others, the word *"dead"* being in the plural. Paul also sees in increased powers a pledge of our own resurrection (1 Cor. 15). Peter sees in it a promise of a heavenly inheritance reserved for us and of our being reserved for it. We are begotten again to a living hope by the resurrection of Jesus Christ from the dead (1 Pet. 1:3-5). John is anxious, both in his Gospel and Revelation, that we distinguish between the resurrection of life and the resurrection of judgment that result from His rising.

We see anticipations of His rising in the Old Testament, not simply in the prophecies that went before Him, but in the types. We shall notice some of these and then go on to the Gospel records themselves. These accounts are as deeply significant as they are charming in simplicity.

The authors, as we have said, seem to be as careless about the difficulties they are creating in the apparent discrepancies in their narratives as they seem unaware of the proofs they are giving of utter absence of collusion between them. We believe each Gospel writer has the mind of God in what he includes and that it is in keeping with the purpose of the book as a whole.

One might imagine in reading Mark's account that the events of the resurrection occupied but a single day, culminating in our Lord's ascension. His frequent use of the word *"after"* does not denote the absence of days. Luke, too, compresses the events into what could conceivably have happened within a day or two. Matthew suggests a longer time in our Lord's later appointment in Galilee, and leaves Jesus on earth. It is John who records things a week apart in the same room, and who *"after these things"* gives details of the appearance in Galilee. It is in Luke's second book that we read that the appearances covered forty days (Acts 1:3).

John's Gospel, written last and so evidently for the Church, furnishes us with most for this age and for our hearts. It shows us that this wonderful event is the cure for friendlessness, fearfulness, and faithlessness as recorded in chapter 20 and for fruitlessness as seen in chapter 21. These human weaknesses are with us today, when they should be with the death shroud in His tomb. Lazarus came forth with the graveclothes on: he would need them again. Our Lord left them behind. So should we, as risen with Him.

May He lead us into the glories of His rising.

Contents

GLIMPSES *of* *the* GLORY

ONE

The Witness of the Wagons

My beloved is like a roe or a young hart: behold, he standeth behind our wall, he looketh forth at the windows, showing himself *through the lattice.*
SONG OF SOLOMON 2:9

He showed Himself *alive after His passion.*
ACTS 1:3

In the Old Testament the story of His rising is latent, as it is patent in the New. Christ not only died for our sins according to the Scriptures, but rose again according to these same sacred writings (1 Cor. 15:3).

These references are to the Old Testament and not to the New, which as yet was scarcely begun when Paul wrote. These Scriptures constitute Exhibit One in the seven witnesses which the apostle brings forward in his great treatise on resurrection. Our Lord's rising was a matter of Old Testament prediction and expectation.

These glimpses of the glory of His rising are not only seen in direct prophecy and in the types, but our Lord shows His face through the lattice of the biographies that went before Him. Apostolic preaching as seen in the Acts draws attention to the fulfillment of prophecy and to the purpose of our Lord's resurrection.

Peter says it was a fulfillment of Psalm 16 and of Psalm 110, the words not referring to David himself, who saw corruption and was not exalted to heaven (Acts 2:25, 36). We are shown the *"path of life"* in Christ's rising. The iron did not bind Him to the tree, nor could He be held by the cords of death. The quotation from Psalm 110 shows the resurrection to be assumed in the eternal priesthood of the One who was David's Lord (see Mt. 22:42). Peter quotes Psalm 118:22 in his address to the Sanhedrin in proof that the rejected stone was to become the Cornerstone (Acts 4:11).

Paul, preaching in the synagogue in Antioch of Pisidia, quotes the second Psalm and shows that the words, *"Thou art My Son, this day have I begotten Thee"* refer not to His birth but to His resurrection. In this psalm the Son is God's King. In Psalm 16 David is a prophet, but he is clearly writing of a greater prophet, like Moses, whom God would raise up. In Psalm 110, our Lord is a Priest—a priest forever. Israel might crucify Him but God will set Him on the holy hill of Zion. Paul also quoted Isaiah 55. The great gospel blessings depicted by Isaiah for all, on the easiest possible terms and reaching on to full millennial blessing, are the sure mercies of David made good by Christ's resurrection.

To these prophecies, quoted by Peter and Paul, might be added others, as the second halves of Psalm 22 and Isaiah 53, where we are led on from death to resurrection. In the Psalms of the cross we exchange the *"roaring"* of the forsaken One for His singing in the midst of the congregation. In an ever-widening circle we see the once forsaken One in the center of an adoring host, the church (v. 22), the seed of Jacob (v. 23), and all the ends of the earth (v. 27). In Isaiah 53, He who was cut off from the land of the living, prolongs His days, and the pleasure of the Lord prospers in His hand (v. 10).

Equally significant are the types, such as the sheaf of firstfruits, which, waved on the first day of the week, becomes a type of Christ the firstfruits, alive from the dead, and the pledge of a harvest to follow (1 Cor. 15:20, 23). The ark of the covenant going down into Jordan, remaining until the safety of the people was assured and then coming out of it, is typical of the true ark of God, Jesus Christ our Lord, through whom the old things of the wilderness pass away, and the new things of the heavenly inheritance will be realized (Josh. 3-4; Eph. 2).

Offerings sacrificed in Israel sometimes involved two victims, as, on the great Day of Atonement (Lev. 16) and the cleansing of the leper (Lev. 14), in which one was killed and the other sent away or set free. Both were necessary to portray in type the death and resurrection of the only One who can cleanse men defiled by the leprosy of sin and take away the sin of a nation.

But it is to some of the biographical foreshadowings,

that we especially turn for glimpses of His rising, to Isaac, to Jonah, to Joseph, and to Daniel.

Isaac: *"I and the lad will go yonder and worship, and come again to you"* (Gen 22:5). Thus did Abraham declare his faith in resurrection. He knew that God had commanded that he offer up his son on one of the mountains, but he accounted *"that God was able to raise him up, even from the dead; from whence also He received him in a figure"* (Heb. 11:19).

Note the references to *"the place"* in Genesis 22. They look forward to *"the place...called Calvary"* (Lk. 23:33). This son of Abraham, miraculously born, whose birth was heralded by an angel, named before his birth, and offered upon Mount Moriah, affords a glimpse of the birth and death and rising again of our Lord. Isaac, afterward coming from his father's house, met his bride in the open air and conducted her home. Rebekah was the fruit of the will of the father, the work of the servant, and the waiting of the son. To this she added her own willingness to respond to the message and gifts of the servant. She is a type of the Bride of Christ, the fruit of the planning and procuring of the triune God.

Jonah: Jonah, too, furnishes us with an anticipation of our Lord's rising from the dead. This prophet of Gath-hepher in Galilee seems to give the lie to those who said, *"Out of Galilee ariseth no prophet"* (Jn. 7:52; 2 Ki. 14:25). His disobedience was not apparently his unwillingness to preach to Gentiles, but to lose face as a prophet if they should believe his message and turn to the Lord, with the inevitable divine mercy for which Jehovah was traditionally famous. But his three days and three nights in the belly of the great fish, from which he emerged to send forth his message, is taken by our Lord to anticipate His own burial and rising again.

While resurrection is not mentioned in Matthew 12, the *"sign of the prophet Jonah"* (v. 39) is that He who was in the depths of the sea, came out of it. The sufferings of Jonah in the great fish are described in language identical with the prophetic cries of the Messiah in Psalm 42:7 and Psalm 69:1. Whether Jonah actually died and was raised, and thus became more fully a type of Christ, is disputable, depending on whether you view his reference to hell (*sheol,* grave) as figurative or literal.

We would, however, examine more fully incidents in the lives of two who, most of all, appear to shadow the life of our Lord. We refer to Joseph and Daniel. These men, appearing at the beginning and toward the close of the canon of the Old Testament, stand for purity amid the polluted atmosphere of Egypt and Babylon. They both discovered that they who live godly shall suffer persecution. Each passed through the crucible of plot and punishment, but both rose to pre-eminence over it and enjoyed future prosperity. Both are interpreters of dreams, both prophets of good things to come.

THE WITNESS OF THE WAGONS

They went up out of Egypt, and came into the land of Canaan
unto Jacob their father, and told him, saying, Joseph is yet alive,

and he is governor over all the land of Egypt. And Jacob's heart fainted, for he believed them not. And they told him all the words of Joseph, which he had said to them: and when he saw the wagons which Joseph had sent to carry him, the spirit of Jacob their father revived: and Israel said, It is enough; Joseph my son is yet alive: I will go and see him before I die (Gen. 45:25-28).

We know of no more suitable portion of the Old Testament on which to preach a resurrection message than this. It combines all the admixture of fear and joy, of uncertainty and assurance that we find in the account of the resurrection of Jesus. The dictum that Old Testament history is *His story* is nowhere more true than in the story of Joseph. He is the Sirius of the shining host of typical men.

We see him introduced in Genesis 37 as the beloved son of the father who left Hebron (fellowship) to go after his brethren. He came unto his own but they received him not. They hated him, particularly because of his dreams, which were portentous and suggested that things in heaven and earth were delivered into his hands. They sold him, at the suggestion of Judah, for silver. Unjustly charged, he was cast into prison. *"Whose feet they hurt with fetters: he was laid in iron"* (Ps. 105:18).

To two men in the prison with him, a butler and a baker, Joseph became a savor—of life to one and of death to the other. The butler who, in his dream, brought of the vine to the king, was accepted. The baker brought his baking—the *"works of the baker,"* says the Bible—and was rejected. His offering never reached the king.

Joseph was then exalted, given a new name, before which all Egypt bows the knee and acknowledged him lord of all.

In all this we see a foreshadowing of the One who was to come, Jesus Christ our Lord. From that perfect fellowship of the Father's house He came to His own. They hated Him without a cause and particularly for His claims. *"All things are delivered unto Me of My Father"* (Mt. 11:27). *"All power is given unto Me in heaven and in earth"* (Mt. 28:18). The betrayal and selling by Judas; the cross where they hurt His feet with fetters, where two men shared His punishment, are all the substance of these shadows in Joseph. One thief pressed the blood of the True Vine into his eager cup when he cried, *"Lord, remember me when Thou comest into Thy kingdom."* He laid hold of the Vine on that day when our Lord became the savor of life unto life in the one who believed, and no less a savor of death unto death in the one who perished (see 2 Cor. 2:14-17).

> *God also hath highly exalted Him, and given Him a name which is above every name: That at the name of Jesus every knee should bow...and that every tongue should confess that Jesus Christ is Lord, to the glory of God the Father* (Phil. 2:9-11).

In all this we see our Beloved showing Himself through the lattice of Old Testament biography.

In Genesis 45, from which we quoted at the beginning, we see the time when Joseph made himself known to his brethren, and bade them carry to his father the news of his existence and exultation. Let us note five important facts about this.

1. An unlikely story: *"Joseph is yet alive, and he is governor over all the land of Egypt."* Joseph had been dead to Jacob for years. *"Joseph is without doubt rent in pieces...I will go down to the grave unto my son mourning,"* were the words of the grief-stricken father as he sat with rent clothes and sackcloth, and with Joseph's blood-stained coat before him. He knew nothing of the treachery and deception of his sons, nor of the nemesis of his own conduct catching up with him at last. He who deceived his father with the skin of a goat is now deceived by his own sons with the blood of a goat.

Neither Jacob nor his sons expected to see Joseph again. Yet here they were, stumbling over one another with descriptions of the exaltation of their brother and the greatness of Egypt. And Joseph had invited them all to come down to him! Though shepherds were an abomination to Egyptians, Joseph had not been ashamed to call them brethren and had presented them to Pharaoh. It was all a strange story, told in eager haste and with shining eyes by the sons of Jacob.

So also is the story of Christ viewed from the human standpoint. From the divine side it has been the subject of Old Testament prophecy and of our Lord's own prediction. It was unlikely to men because they had not grasped these ancient foretellings, and because in the excitement of the events leading up to the cross, they had forgotten the Lord's words. The words of the women early at the sepulcher on the first day of the week, that the grave was empty and that they had seen a vision of angels who said Jesus was alive, were but idle tales to the hearers (Lk. 24:11).

2. An unbelieving heart: *"And Jacob's heart fainted, for he believed them not."* Note the word *"for."* There is nothing so weakening to the heart as unbelief. But how could old Jacob believe such a tale? Over twenty years had gone by. And what about the bloodstained coat? His sons had found it, they had said, in the field. What were they saying now? Were they confessing that they had sold Joseph into slavery? We doubt it. Jacob was not convinced by his sons. He knew them—Reuben, unstable as water; Simeon and Levi, cruel, self-willed, angry men. Joseph had brought back their evil report. Jacob did not believe them.

So it was in the story of the resurrection. Uninspired writers, anxious to buttress a faith, would not have represented the disciples as incredulous, but—with the predictions of the Scriptures and of the Saviour in mind—quietly and confidently waiting the news of His rising. Instead these penmen write of things which seem to militate against faith in the resurrection, even stating that our Lord was not recognized by some of His own. In these matters they manifest that they are true men, trustworthy witnesses.

Mary Magdalene had told the weeping, mourning disciples that she had seen Him alive, but they did not believe her. The Emmaus disciples had returned to

Jerusalem with the glad news, but they were not believed either (Mk. 16:13).

Our Lord upbraided them because of their unbelief. *"Except I shall see...I will not believe,"* (Jn. 20:25) cried Thomas, and languished in his unbelief for a week. The disciples *"were terrified and affrighted, and supposed that they had seen a spirit,"* when Jesus appeared in their midst (Lk. 24:37).

Thus the theory that the followers of Jesus, both men and women, were expecting a resurrection and thereby prepared to "see anything," falls down for want of a vestige of proof in the account. They were not "hysterical women," as Renan says, nor were they gullible men. Unbelieving hearts were everywhere. The incredulity of the disciples seems incredulous to us who, centuries later, review the proceedings in the light of prophecy and history.

3. Unmistakable proof: *"And when he saw the wagons...the spirit of Jacob their father revived"* (v. 27).To the *words* of Joseph urging all his house not to delay in their return to Egypt, these sons added the *work* of Joseph in providing the means of transportation. The proof of their assertion was there. The wagons were the witness and their logic was inescapable. These sons of Jacob led the trembling old man outside and showed him the gilded wagons of Egypt. Doubtless these royal vehicles, with their richly caparisoned Egyptian horses, bore the crests and insignia of Pharaoh. Egypt was proverbial in the raising of horses of beauty and training, and of worthy vehicles to be drawn by them, so that Solomon would give six hundred shekels of silver for a single chariot and a hundred and fifty shekels for a horse (2 Chron. 1:17). These wagons could have come from none other than the mighty Pharaoh. Joseph had given them by command of the king. The proof was inescapable.

In the same way, the disciples of our Lord Jesus Christ had proof, infallible proof, in fact, many infallible proofs (Acts 1:3). The writer of the Acts begins by showing that these disciples had the evidence of their senses.

THEY SAW HIM. Christ *"showed Himself alive after His passion...being seen of them forty days"* (Acts 1:3). He was seen of Cephas (Peter), then of the twelve. After that He was seen of more than five hundred brethren at once (1 Cor. 15:5-6). They had the evidence of their eyes: not one or two seeing Him in the gray light of the morning of that third day, or in the shadows of that same evening, but more than five hundred men seeing Him at the same time at a rendezvous in Galilee.

THEY HEARD HIM. *"Speaking of the things pertaining to the kingdom of God."* These followers of a rejected Messiah heard Him in resurrection; heard not only His commands, but His answers to their questions. *"Lord, wilt Thou at this time restore again the kingdom to Israel?"* was their eager query. In swift reply He answered, *"It is not for you to know the times or the seasons, which the Father hath put in His own power."* They were not deceived. The communications of their Lord were too numerous, too varied, too personal—so person-al that a Peter, a Thomas, a Saul of Tarsus, would never deny or doubt again. In the case of Saul (see Acts 9:1-6), however the title of *"Lord"* might have escaped the lips of that Nazarene-hating Jew at first when a voice from heaven reached his ears, it would not have been repeated after the speaker was self-identified as Jesus. The repeti-tion of the divine title on the part of the erstwhile perse-cutor was the sudden realization of the enormity of his guilt and the sudden declaration of his faith in the resur-rection of Jesus of Nazareth and of his allegiance to Him from that day forward. *"Last of all,"* Paul wrote, *"He was seen of me."* He might have added, "heard of me."

THEY TOUCHED HIM. They were assembled together with Him (Acts 1:4). The margin reads, *"They were eat-ing together with Him."* The word means to throng close-ly together. John records that Jesus gave the disciples bread and fish. They received the food at His hands. Luke records that they gave Him a piece of broiled fish and of a honeycomb. In the Emmaus home our Lord broke the bread and gave to them from it; they had His bread in their hands. Women held Him by the feet (Mt. 28:9). Thomas was invited to thrust his hand into His side (Jn. 20:27). *"Handle Me, and see; for a spirit hath not flesh and bones, as ye see Me have"* (Lk. 24:39). To the evidence of sight was added that of touch.

THEY ATE WITH HIM. *"Come and dine." "Have ye here any meat?"* These were not so much the evidence of His physical hunger as of His physical resurrection. The eating was food for their faith. They had the evidence of taste.

To these four evidences of their senses, we might reverently add the fifth, the sense of smell. God suffered not His Holy One to see corruption. Death had no dominion over Him. There was not a taint, a trace, of the corruption that so soon embraces our beloved dead. *"For David, after he had served his own generation by the will of God, fell on sleep, and was laid unto his fathers, and saw corruption: but He, whom God raised again, saw no corruption"* (Acts 13:36-37).

4. An unqualified admission: *"And Israel said, It is enough; Joseph my son is yet alive"* (Gen. 45:28). The evidence was sufficient for the skeptical Jacob. Believing Israel took over and gave utterance to his faith. Note the change in the names. Jacob's heart fainted, but Israel said the evidence was "abundant," as the word is sometimes translated. Unbelief with its attendant faintness of heart had passed away; faith and strength had come to the aged patriarch.

So also with the disciples of Jesus and with a multitude since who have faced the evidences of resurrection. It was enough for the immediate propagators of the faith, most of whom laid down their lives for it. They faced the same foes before whom they had fled only a few weeks before. The bravest of the disciples had denied his Lord with oaths and curses: now he stands up and charges Israel with denying the Holy and just One.

It was enough for Saul of Tarsus of the tribe of Benjamin who, like his progenitor, had been ravening as a wolf and devouring the prey in the morning of his life but who, in the evening of it, so gladly divided the spoils of his victory (Gen. 49:27). *"Am I not an apostle?... Have I not seen Jesus Christ our Lord? Are not ye my work in the Lord?"* (1 Cor. 9:1). Paul's supreme victory was the knowledge of the Holy One. How greatly he yearned that Christ might be formed in those who were his work in the Lord.

It was enough for the noble company of martyrs, who for their faith endured the rack and the flood and the flame.

It was enough for men like General Lew Wallace, Lord Lyttleton, and Sir Gilbert West, who started to write their books as unbelievers or with the avowed intention of writing against Christianity, but who finished by declaring and defending their faith in Christ.

It was enough for I. H. Linton, author of *A Lawyer and the Bible,* and for Frank Morrison, author of *Who Moved the Stone?* The latter tells us in his introduction that as a youth he rebelled against repeating the Apostles' Creed when it spoke of Christ who was crucified under Pontius Pilate, but raised from the dead. He made up his mind even then that, if he secured an education and had the ability, he would write a book against the doctrine of the resurrection of Jesus. He tells how, as he sat down to write, gathering the data and sifting the evidence, his purpose was changed and he was compelled to write in defense of the faith. For cogency and lucidity this ranks among the best of any modern apologetic on the resurrection of our Lord.

It is enough for the present writer, who rejoices to declare his personal conviction that He who was delivered for his offenses was raised again for his justification on that glorious Easter morning.

And it is enough for us all. The evidence is there. The things that concern Christ's death, burial, and resurrection, were not done in a corner. The tenets of our faith are open to investigation. Our unbelief does not really stem from lack of evidence but from lack of interest or of holiness. God has placed the cardinal fact of Christianity on an unshakable foundation.

5. Undeniable resolve: *"I will go and see him before I die"* (Gen. 45:28). The aged man was ready for the road. We have conceived the possibility of one of Jacob's sons being dubious about the father's ability to stand the long journey to Egypt even in the gilded wagons, only to be strongly assured that the determined old man would walk if necessary. Such an assuring message required an instant response.

Shall we not do the same? We must meet the Saviour in faith before we die if we would "die in faith." We must respond and our faith should be as active and articulate as Jacob's. Let us remember, too, that the world still waits to see the witness of the wagons in us who say that the Saviour of the world, our Joseph, is alive. "Show us a proof," they say, "a promise, a power from that other country you tell us of, where there is bread enough and to spare, and we'll be ready to go. Show us an unworldly life, a joyous countenance. Show us answered prayer in your own life. Show us the fruit of the Spirit, and we shall behold the power, the heavenly chariots to carry us beyond our scene of famine and pain. Show us wagons, those assuring texts of Scripture, those God-breathed vehicles which carry people from doubt to faith, from fear to joy, from abject poverty to fabulous wealth."

Jacob not only talked about going; He went. *"And Israel took his journey with all that he had"* (Gen. 46:1). The names of his sons and their sons who went with Him are recorded, as are the names of those who believe the gospel message concerning Jesus Christ our Lord. Joseph left his palace and came to meet the cavalcade at Goshen, falling upon his father's neck and weeping a good while. Tears came often to Joseph: he is seen weeping seven times in the Genesis record.

Then he goes with them to present them to Pharaoh. He is not ashamed of them, as we have said, though they are shepherds and every shepherd was an abomination to Egyptians. The brethren are accepted in the beloved Joseph.

What a day when our Joseph leaves His ivory palace to meet us in the air to conduct us home! What a day of presentation when we come before God as the brethren of Christ. *"For this cause He is not ashamed to call us brethren, saying, I will declare Thy name unto My brethren, in the midst of the church will I sing praise unto thee"* (Heb. 2:11-12). With our name in the Book of Life, we gladly await that day, that cloudless morning.

Jesus lives, and so shall I.
Death! Thy sting is gone forever!
He who deigned for me to die
Lives, the bands of death to sever.
He shall raise me from the dust;
Jesus is my Hope and Trust.

Jesus lives and death is now
But my entrance into glory.
Courage then, my soul, for thou
Hast a crown of life before thee;
Thou shalt find thy hopes were just;
Jesus is the Christian's trust.

—CHRISTIAN F. GELLERT

TWO

Weighed but not Wanting

*The king commanded, and they brought Daniel, and cast
him into the den of lions. Now the king spake and said
unto Daniel, Thy God whom thou servest continually,
He will deliver thee. And a stone was brought, and laid
upon the mouth of the den; and the king sealed it with
his own signet, and with the signet of his lords; that the
purpose might not be changed concerning Daniel...
Then the king rose very early in the morning, and went
in haste unto the den of lions... Daniel was taken up out
of the den, and no manner of hurt was found upon him,
because he believed in his God.* DANIEL 6:16-23

*Pilate said unto them, Ye have a watch: go your way,
make it as sure as ye can. So they went, and made the
sepulcher sure, sealing the stone, and setting a watch.*
MATTHEW 27:65-66

Save me from the lion's mouth.
PSALM 22:21

Very early in the morning the first day of the week,
they came unto the sepulcher at the rising of the sun.
MARK 16:2

He, whom God raised again, saw no corruption.
ACTS 13:37

Here once again we have glimpses of the glory of His rising. Daniel chapter 5 contrasts greatly with chapter 6. In the former there is a king who is weighed in the balances and who is *"found wanting"*; the second is a ruler of his kingdom who is found faultless (v. 4), *"found... praying"* (v. 11), found innocent (v. 22), and found unhurt (v. 23). Chapter 5 sums up the teaching of the Bible concerning man; chapter 6 sums it up concerning Christ. When weighed in the balances, not of public opinion nor of personal estimation, but in the scale of God, with the ten weights of His holy commandments, man is weighed and found wanting.

From ancient Babylon, archeology recovered a portrayal of the "weighing of the heart in the hall of the double truth," showing that the Babylonians believe in a future weighing of the intents of the heart.

Recently, in the British Museum, we saw on a mural the Egyptian equivalent of this. Ani and Thuthu enter the hall of judgment. Anubis weighs the hearts in the balances, first testing them, while Thoth records the results. The "Eater of the Dead" waits wolfishly to eat condemned hearts. But Ani and Thuthu are justified and led into the presence of Osiris, where they kneel down and worship.

It was a surprise for Belshazzar, the king, to discover that he had already been weighed and was wanting. Weighed by the law of God which is holy, just, and good, man has been declared guilty before God. Belshazzar had been no better than his grandfather, Nebuchadnezzar. That despotic monarch had the power of life and death in his own hands within his kingdom. Whom he would, he slew, and whom he would, he kept alive. But he had been humbled, deposed, deprived of his glory, driven out from men. He had become deranged in mind and had his dwelling with the beasts.

But all this had wrought no change in Belshazzar though it had in the heart of Nebuchadnezzar himself. His testimony to the change is given in Daniel 4:34-37. Belshazzar had not humbled himself, though he knew all that had happened to his predecessor on the throne. He had not glorified God.

In chapter 6, however, there is a man who does, and who becomes a type of Him who was able to say, *"I have glorified Thee on earth"* (Jn. 17:4).

Let us trace these likenesses to Christ in the ancient record of Daniel, whose long life spanned the reigns of the ever-changing monarchs of Babylon: Nebuchadnezzar, Nabonides, Belshazzar, Darius the Median, and Cyrus the Persian.

Daniel is like Christ in his position and preferment. Daniel had been made third ruler in the kingdom by order of Belshazzar. With this king evidently ruling as viceroy in the absence of his father, Nabonides, who was out on conquest and later a prisoner, Daniel was the third ruler. He had gone from honor to honor in Babylon, in spite of the fact that he did not conform to the ways of the court of Babylon. He *"purposed in his heart that he would not defile himself with the king's meat, nor with the wine which he drank"* (Dan. 1:8), and at the end of ten days he and his friends were *"found better,"* both in appearance and in knowledge, than the wise men of the realm. He was made great and received many honors at the beginning of this book (Dan. 2:48). He was further honored after his refusal to make petition to Belshazzar, and he was honored by Darius, being made chief of the hundred and twenty princes set over the whole kingdom, and of three presidents set over these princes. It was in the king's mind to set Daniel over everything; he was preferred above all.

In all this we see the position of Jesus Christ our Lord.

He it is, who coming after Me, is preferred before Me, whose shoe's latchet I am not worthy to unloose... This is He of whom I said, After Me cometh a man which is preferred before me, for He was before Me (Jn. 1:27, 30).

These verses occur in a chapter redolent with divine attributes and names of Christ. He is the Eternal Word, the True Light, the Lamb of God, the Son of God, the King of Israel, the Son of Man. John the Baptist was before Him in birth, but the Son was before John in life. He was in the beginning with God but was made flesh and dwelt among us. Truly His position was great, His power divine.

Daniel is like Christ in his piety and purity. It was not simply that Daniel lived before men in purity; he lived before God in piety. He had power with God in prayer, and was faithful and without fault with men. He not only had the windows of his house open toward Jerusalem, he had ever the window of his heart open toward Jehovah. This man, found faultless, was found praying. To his set times of prayer, three times a day, were added special times of supplication when he apparently did nothing else. He understood by books that the end of the captivity of Israel was near, but set himself to pray as if his prayer alone was the cause of the fulfillment of the prophecy. He was a man *"greatly beloved"* of God (Dan. 10:11). He would not defile himself with the king's meat, nor obey the command to cease making his requests known to God. And he disclaimed any wisdom of his own in making known the king's dream.

How much he reminds us of the One who was holy, harmless, undefiled, and separate from sinners.

HE WAS HOLY TOWARD GOD. He always had an eye first of all for the glory of God. He was often found praying.

HE WAS HARMLESS BEFORE MEN. His gentleness made Him great.

HE WAS UNDEFILED IN HIMSELF, not only without fault, but without sin.

HE WAS SEPARATE FROM SINNERS, never walking in the counsel of the ungodly, nor standing in the way of sinners, nor sitting in the seat of the scornful. He was the fruitful Man of Psalm 1, who became the forsaken Man of Psalm 22, in order that the filthy man of Psalm 14 might become the forgiven man of Psalm 32. He did always the things that pleased the Father, the One greatly beloved by Him. *"This is My beloved Son"* (Mt. 3:17).

Daniel is like Christ in the plot and the punishment against him. His enemies knew that they could not find occasion against Daniel in the administration of the affairs of the kingdom of Babylon. They could only hope to get him in conflict with the king himself. The law of the king must be found to be in conflict with the law of Daniel's God. Hence the cunning plot of the presidents and the princes.

The autocratic, despotic kingdom of Babylon had given place to the Medo-Persian, and the deterioration was manifest. The head of gold in Nebuchadnezzar's vision had indeed given place to the breast and arms of silver. Like Ahasuerus in the book of Esther, this Darius was a mere pawn in the hands of his rulers. His edicts were but the clever plots of his counselors, nor could he alter his own decrees. Whom he would he could not keep alive, unlike the first Babylonian king.

When the plot was discovered, Darius was sorely displeased, not with Daniel, but with himself. He could perceive that for envy they had delivered Daniel to the unalterable laws of the Medes and Persians. He set his heart to deliver him, but labored in vain. Love was helpless in the presence of law. The punishment must be carried out; Daniel must be cast into the den of lions. Nor could he get out. A stone was brought and laid on the mouth of the den, and sealed with the seals of both the king and his lords. No one was to break the seal; the purpose must not be changed (Dan. 6:17).

So also with our Lord Jesus Christ. *"I find no fault in Him,"* declared Pilate again and again. When it looked as if the Jews might lose their case against Christ, they put Him in conflict with the king, with Caesar. *"He that maketh himself a king, speaketh against Caesar."* The charge was quickly changed to a political one. Nothing could be proved against Jesus as to His character; false charges must be made through His claims. He made Himself a king, they said: *"We have no king but Caesar."* Pilate *"knew that for envy they had delivered Him"* (Mt. 27:18). The governor labored to deliver Jesus, but, ignoring the pleading of his wife, yielded to the demands of the rulers of Israel. Jesus must be crucified.

"Save me from the lion's mouth." The words occur in Psalm 22, the psalm of the Cross. In the midst of three hostile circles is heard the orphan cry of Emmanuel. Beset by the savage beasts of humanity, the bulls of Bashan, who are evidently the oppressive lords of Israel (Amos 4:1); by the rapacious dogs of the Gentiles; and by the assembly of the wicked one, our Lord's cry is heard. The roaring of the lion mingles with the *"roaring"* of the One forsaken by God.

By contrast, how blessed to see Him, the Lion of the tribe of Judah, in the midst of three adoring circles in Revelation 5. The angels gather about the throne, the living creatures, and the four and twenty elders unite to say with a loud voice, *"Worthy is the Lamb that was slain."*

Daniel is like Christ in his pre-eminence and his prosperity. An angel closed the mouths of the lions. Now the king himself gladly breaks the seal and rolls the stone away. The law has been vindicated and is now helpless in the presence of love. Daniel must be freed and his accusers judged. Then follows a universal proclamation. All nations, peoples, and languages are sent a message of peace and commanded to tremble and fear before the God of Daniel. A decree from the king had given Daniel to the lions; a new decree would honor his God. The "resurrected" prophet was proof of His power. As for Daniel, he continued in prosperity.

Thus is foreshadowed the triumph of Christ. The angel of the Lord breaks the seal and rolls away the stone. He sits upon it in supreme disdain for the decrees of men. The stone was not rolled away to let the Saviour out: it was to show the tomb was empty. A world-wide proclamation followed His rising. *"Go ye into all the world, and preach the gospel to every creature." "The pleasure of the Lord"* prospers in the hand of that resurrected Man. *"Therefore will I divide Him a portion with the great, and He shall divide the spoil with the strong; because He hath poured out His soul unto death"* (Isa. 53:10-12). The result of that proclamation is the drawing of all to Him. *"I, if I be lifted up from [out of] the earth, will draw all men unto Me"* (Jn. 12:32). It is not simply His crucifixion that draws; it is the glory of His rising. Thus He looks forth at the windows, showing Himself through the lattice of Old Testament biography.

We have read of a traveling man who brought home to

his children a large jigsaw puzzle. When properly pieced together it formed a map of a certain country. Thinking it would keep them busy for a long time in finding the pieces and identifying the country, he was surprised when they called to him in a short time and stated that it was complete. When he asked the secret, they told him that there was a man's face on the other side of the map, the face of a king, so they put the face together and the difficult task of matching the pieces of the map was taken away. So it is with the seeming task of seeing harmony in the pieces of Old Testament history, prophecy, biography, poetry, and ceremony, that form the ancient and earlier division of the Bible. When you discover that back of everything is the face of a Man who is a King, you see plan and purpose in it all. To Him they all give witness, and among the events they portray none is so prominent and precious as the glimpses of the glory of His rising again from the dead.

> *Thine be the glory, risen, conqu'ring Son,*
> *Endless is the vict'ry Thou o'er death hast won;*
> *Angels in bright raiment rolled the stone away,*
> *Kept the folded grave clothes, where Thy body lay.*
>
> *Lo! Jesus meets us, risen from the tomb;*
> *Lovingly He greets us, scatters fear and gloom;*
> *Let the Church with gladness hymns of triumph sing,*
> *For her Lord now liveth; death has lost its sting.*

—EDMOND L. BUDRY

The WITNESS of JOHN

The Message to the Church

THREE

The New Things of Christianity

When He had so said, He showed unto them His hands
and His side. Then were the disciples glad,
when they saw the Lord.
MATTHEW 16:21

The Gospel of John furnishes us with much that the earlier records do not, particularly in the individual audiences of our Lord. While other Gospels lead up to the rejection of Christ, John begins with it. At the end of his book he assures us that his is but a sample list of the mighty signs of his Lord. In his resurrection scenes John brings in much that the others do not, things which are distinctively for the present period of the Church. They are the new things of Christianity at which we should take a closer look.

We have the new day, the first day of the week, the

distinctive day of Christianity. John gives a new proof of resurrection—something the other evangelists do not record—the undisturbed graveclothes of Jesus our Lord. We have a new relationship indicated in the message of those now designated as His *"brethren,"* a relationship not of earth, for He was ascending to His Father and their Father, to His God and their God. Not "our Father and our God," for He is ever, like the wrappings about His head in the tomb, in a place by Himself. A new people with new privileges is indicated in His breathing on them and imparting the Holy Spirit, with authority conferred upon them to remit and retain sins. A new principle, that which characterizes the present age, is that we walk not by sight, as Israel, but by faith. *"Blessed are they,"* said our Lord, *"that have not seen, and yet have believed"* (Jn. 20:29).

John closes this section with the clear purpose of his writing. It is not simply, as with Luke, that we might know the certainty of the things surely believed among us, but that we might believe that Jesus is the Son of God, and believing, have life through His Name. We shall take up these new things of Christianity in this chapter. They reveal some of the glories of His rising.

Let us notice in John's writing that, when our Lord expired, Joseph of Arimathea and Nicodemus are joined in open and consecrated service to do honor to Christ. Joseph brings the linen, Nicodemus the spices. It is singular that Joseph, who lived twenty miles away, should have a sepulcher at Jerusalem—not in the city where

others besides kings were buried (2 Chron. 21:20;
24:25), but outside the city at the place of the skull. This
rich man evidently owned the garden and the tomb.
While the resurrection made the disciples bold (Acts
4:13), the death of Jesus was the occasion for which
Joseph and Nicodemus had waited and planned, when
they boldly came forward to sever their link with the
Sanhedrin and the temple. Everything was evidently
ready for the burying of our Lord—perhaps even the
garden tomb purchased for Him and hewn personally by
the hand of Joseph.

Perhaps we do him an injury by saying that he was a
secret disciple for fear of the Jews. The word seems to
mean "secreted," forced to hide, it may be, because of
plots on his life. He could scarcely have been afraid of
losing his position in the Sanhedrin, seeing he now
appeared on our Lord's behalf. Nor could he be afraid of
not being able to participate in the temple service, being
a chief man among his people (Lev. 21:4), seeing he was
handling a dead body on the eve of the Passover.

In company with Nicodemus he had prepared the
linen, the spices, and the tomb. Jesus would have the
first place in it, the virgin place in the tomb as in the
womb. These consecrated men would carry forth the
burnt offering to *"a clean place"* (Lev. 6:10-11). As in
the type, these men *"changed their garments and put on
other garments."* They had renounced the old and put on
the new—going forth themselves *"unto Him without the
camp, bearing His reproach"* (Heb. 13:13).

In their loving ministry to their Lord they give witness

to the reality of His death. Pilate inquired of the centurion before he gave Joseph permission to take away the body (Mk. 15:44-45). Jesus was really dead. Now He was really alive; He showed Himself.

A new period of grace: It was the first day of the week (Jn. 20:1). The Sabbath stood at the end of the working week and was the reward of labor well done. The Jewish leaders rushed our Lord to death in order to keep a Sabbath. Their labor culminated with the murder of the Son of God. There could be no rest for them.

The first day of the week was the new day for the Church. Its significance is clearly anticipated in the Old Testament. (See Lev. 23, where the sacred days in the calendar of Israel are indicated.) Both the Firstfruits and Pentecost are on the morrow after the Sabbath. These *"feasts of the Lord"* are evidently divided into four and three, the first four occurring at the beginning of the sacred year, followed by a considerable period between. The last three follow in quick succession. The pause in between answers to the present period of grace.

Christ the firstfruits and the birthday of the Church are the fulfillment of the types. Both occur on the first day of the week. The new day inaugurates the new dispensation. The Sabbath was a sign between God and the children of Israel (Ex. 31:17). It was part of the shadows passing away with the coming of the substance, the things concerning Christ (Col. 2:16-17). A slain Messiah in a grave on the Sabbath was all that Israel could do under law; a risen Lord on the first day of the week marked a new beginning. On this day the Church was born, people baptized, the Lord's Supper enjoyed, the collection made (Acts 2:1, 41-42; 20:7 1 Cor. 16:2).*

A new proof of resurrection:

And he stooping down, and looking in, saw the linen clothes lying...and the napkin, that was about His head, not lying with the linen clothes, but wrapped together in a place by itself. Then went in also that other disciple, which came first to the sepulcher, and he saw, and believed (Jn. 20:5-8).

The appearance of the grave clothes of our Lord was evidently convincing proof to John of resurrection. He was spectator to it all. When Mary Magdalene brought the news of the empty tomb, Peter and John ran to the grave. Peter with characteristic confidence may have thought he could outrun John, but was left behind by the disciple whom Jesus loved. John uses three different words to describe the seeing of that morning. Coming first, he had not gone in, but saw, in the gray light of the tomb, the clothes lying. A moment later Peter had come up and gone in and saw more closely, noting that the head covering was not mingled with the other clothes, but wrapped by itself. To Peter the coverings may simply have indicated the deliberation of the most recent occupant of the tomb. There was no frightful haste as of men

* Excerpted from *Sunday—Not Saturday—the Day for the Church,* Neil Fraser, Faithful Words Publishing Company, St. Louis, MO.

engaged in the clandestine removal of the body. But John, coming in after Peter, *"saw"* and believed. He perceived the significance. There was design as well as deliberation. The clothes were in their original convolutions. To John it was irresistible proof of the resurrection.

"Come, see the place where the Lord lay." The angel's words to the women early at the sepulcher would take on new meaning afterwards. If friends had removed the body, as sleeping guards testified later, they would have reverently kept the body covered. If foes had removed it, they would not have taken time to wrap up the clothes in orderly fashion. Our Lord left the cerements behind.

Note that this external proof did not activate these disciples as the ministry of the Lord would do to the Emmaus disciples. Here we read that as yet they had not grasped the Scriptures that spoke of His rising (v. 9). Therefore they went away again to their own home (v. 10). On the other hand the Emmaus-bound disciples got a ministry of Christ from *"Moses and all the prophets."* Their heart burned within them. The *"stranger unawares"* they had entertained could only be the Lord! *"And they rose up the same hour, and returned to Jerusalem"* (Lk. 24:27-33).

External proofs have their place in Christianity. The things were not done in a comer. Its revelation does not consist in golden plates covered with writing, falling from heaven before the eyes of a lone man, and as mysteriously received up to heaven again. Its tenets are open to investigation and can be defended. But Dr. F. W.

Boreham of Australia tells us that in reading over hundreds of volumes on the conversion of men of eminence, he was surprised to find that the majority of these hardheaded, unemotional men were not won to Christ by an unanswerable argument, but by a sudden appreciation of the wonders of divine love. They entered the kingdom of God, not through their heads, but through their hearts. Paul places the evidence of the Holy Scriptures before the evidences of sight in his witness to the resurrection in 1 Corinthians 15. Peter and John returned to their homes after the external evidence, the evidence of sight, the two from Emmaus left their home to tell others after the ministry of the Scriptures to their hearts.

A new place of favor: *"Go to My brethren, and say unto them, I ascend unto My Father, and your Father; and to My God, and your God"* (Jn. 20:17). In this Gospel, Jesus spoke to His own as *"My sheep"* and *"My friends."* Here it is *"My brethren."* He is not ashamed to call us brethren (Heb. 2:11-12). This close place of favor was not knowledge after the flesh. He was ascending to God the Father, both His and theirs. They were all of one. It was a place consequent upon His ascension.

We do not think there was an ascension to heaven that day to "present the blood in the holiest in fulfillment of the type," as some suggest, with a return made to earth that evening. The words, *"Touch Me not, for I am not yet ascended to My Father,"* would rather correct the false assumption of Mary that He had returned to earth in fulfillment of His own words, *"I will come again and receive you unto Myself."* He had not ascended to the Father's house, much less returned. The scripture was not yet fulfilled, *"Sit Thou on My right hand."* The fact that later the disciples held Him by the feet shows there was no particular significance in the physical act at that time. The earthly relationship was set aside; the closer spiritual tie was in effect. His own were His brethren; His Father was their Father. This nearness and dearness we but dimly apprehend here. *"Both He that sanctifieth and they that are sanctified are all of one, for which cause He is not ashamed to call them brethren"* (Heb. 2:11).

A new people of God: *"He breathed on them, and saith unto them, Receive ye the Holy Ghost."* This also is peculiar to John. The word *"breathed"* is a new word, used nowhere else in the New Testament, but in the Septuagint of Genesis 2:7: *"God formed man of the dust of the ground, and breathed into his nostrils the breath of life."* That was in the old creation; this was in the new. The prerogatives of God in Genesis 2 are the prerogatives of the Son in John 20. The first man Adam was made a living soul; the last Adam was a life-giving Spirit (1 Cor. 15:45). *"For as the Father hath life in Himself; so hath He given to the Son to have life in Himself"* (Jn. 5:26). In Ezekiel 37, God the Spirit breathes and Israel is born anew. With the breath of His lips shall Antichrist and his satellites be slain (2 Thess. 2:8; Isa. 11:4).

The breathing of John 20 we judge was not therefore a bestowal of power which must await Pentecost, but a bestowal of authority to act for Him in the new order.

The first breathing brought forth the human race; the last would bring the chosen race to new life after their bones had been dry and dead. The one between brings forward the heavenly people. Typical of Christianity is the indwelling Spirit. Having believed, we are sealed with the Spirit of God (Eph. 1:13).

The new privilege of service: *"Whose soever sins ye remit, they are remitted unto them; and whose soever sins ye retain, they are retained"* (Jn. 20:22-23). That this was a privilege extended not to the eleven only, but also to *"those that were with them,"* is clear from Luke 24:33. The privileges here are not confined to some supposed apostolic succession, but are the common portion of all thus indwelt by the Spirit. There is a similar passage in Matthew 18:18 in connection with discipline in the future church of which Jesus spoke. There the binding comes first, the erring person being bound over by the church and the decision ratified in heaven. The loosing or forgiving of the person upon his repentance comes later, which restoration to fellowship is noted in heaven. *"To whom ye forgive anything, I forgive also…in the person of Christ"* (2 Cor. 2:10). This Paul wrote in connection with the restoration of the excommunicated member in Corinth.

Here in John, however, the order is evangelical. The Lord is sending out His disciples with the message of peace. *"As My Father hath sent Me, even so send I you."* The remission comes first. The retaining would only be as a consequence of unbelief. Representatives of Christ carry out this privilege when they go forth in His Name, bringing the message of forgiveness and peace to others. To the one who receives the gospel, purchased by the blood of the Cross, there is remission; to him who refuses, a message of retention. He is still in his sins, and is the more guilty now that he has heard. On the authority of the Master, the servant assures the repentant one that, having believed in the Lord Jesus Christ, he is forgiven. By the same authority he tells the unrepentant that his sins are upon him. We bind and loose in the Church when we act in discipline for Christ the Head; we loose and retain when we act for Him in the world in the proclamation of His message of peace.

The priest of old had this authoritative declaration in connection with the leper. He officially pronounced him unclean when the disease was apparent. If God came in and cleansed the leper, he was pronounced clean by the priest (Lev. 13:14-15; 14:7). The priest did not cleanse the leper; he pronounced him clean. In the same way we do not cleanse the sinner; we declare forgiveness to the believing soul, but none to him who persists in unbelief.

A new principle of life: *"Blessed are they that have not seen, and yet have believed"* (Jn. 20:29). Thomas was a true representative of his people. They walked by sight. Their promises of the law for obedience were material, a man's very health and wealth normally proclaiming his favor of the Lord. All this was promised to Israel (Deut. 28:1-13). Thomas said, *"Except I see...I will not believe"* (Jn. 20:25). Seeing was believing.

In contrast to this, our Lord inaugurated the period of faith. Believing is seeing. *"Said I not unto thee, If thou wouldst believe, thou shouldest see the glory of God."* Thomas would stand on the old ground of sight; our Lord showed him the new principle, the heavenly basis of faith. The sight of Christ's wounds removed his doubts, as they will the unbelief of Israel in a day to come. In this age, *"we walk by faith, not by sight."*

Things that could be seen characterized the entire old economy. There was a place where God put His Name and where only He was to be worshiped. There is no such particular place in the New Testament. To say that any of us has the only place where God can be reached, is to err. The apostles of Christ make no mention of a certain place where the Church meets. The Person is everything; the place, wherever two or three meet in His Name. This is the dispensation not of the place, but of the Person; not of the ritual, but of the Spirit; not of things seen, but of faith in things unseen.

Happy are they who do not see, yet trust. They may not understand their present circumstances, the pain, the sorrow, the bereavement, but they believe the Lord knows and cares. Their faith is in One whom, having not seen, they love. They *"endure as seeing Him who is invisible." "They look for a city whose builder and maker is God."* In this venture of faith they choose *"rather to suffer affliction with the people of God, than to enjoy the pleasures of sin for a season."* They have *"respect unto the recompense of the reward."* These quotations are from a chapter (Heb. 11) that deals with the triumph of faith. There we see that it is by faith that we understand (v. 3); by faith we undertake (vv. 4-41); and by faith we undergo (vv. 32-40). There we see that despite the intervening earthly promises, God's "hall of fame" is covered with portraits of men and women who walked by faith and not by sight. We see there a faith that delivers a proper child, a faith that defies a king's decree, a faith that decides a future destiny, a faith that discerns the will of God at long last, a faith that desires a better country. We see faith exercised before birth, at birth, in maturity, in old age, and at the point of death. There is no time, no sphere where it may not operate in our lives.

Thrice blessed is he who has not seen, yet has believed; who lives his life today in the light of tomorrow; who weighs his actions and ambitions and achievements, not in the balance of human approbation, but in the balance of the sanctuary; who knows that the world passes away, but he who does the will of God abides forever.

A new purpose in writing: *"These are written, that ye might believe that Jesus is the Christ, the Son of God; and that believing ye might have life through His name"* (Jn. 20:31). The object of Matthew and Mark in writing their Gospels is plainly seen but not declared. Luke, however, tells us in his introduction that, having accurate knowledge of all things from the very first concerning Jesus, he was setting down in orderly fashion a declaration of those things firmly believed among us. How much we are indebted to Luke the physician for his story of the virgin birth and his sympathetic portrayal of so many things unnoted in the earlier writings. But John declares his avowed purpose is that we might believe in Him whom he presents, though John himself never urges us to do so. His purpose is an evangelical one: he deals with the truth of life, light, and love as seen in Jesus. His Epistles deal with the test of life, and light, and love as seen in God's people. His Revelation deals with the triumph of these things. John has the privilege of writing in all three divisions of the New Testament, in the historical, didactic, and prophetic portions. His Gospel is essentially evangelical and Christian. The Upper Room discourse, which John alone records, shows the ecclesiastical aspect of the return of Christ, as the Olivet message in Matthew shows the larger view of His coming in relation to Israel, Christendom, and the nations.

The Upper Room message was spoken to those who would form the nucleus of the Church; the Olivet discourse to the same disciples who one day would sit on twelve thrones, judging the tribes of Israel.

These new things of John 20 help us to delineate the present dispensation.

FOUR

The Risen Christ: the Cure

In the twentieth chapter of John, the risen Christ is the cure for the friendlessness of Mary (vv. 1-18), for the fearfulness of the disciples (vv. 19-23), and for the faithlessness of Thomas (vv. 24-29). In chapter 21, He is the cure for fruitlessness, when we toil all the night and take nothing. Christ shows Himself the answer for these weaknesses of men.

Friendlessness: Mary stood outside the sepulcher weeping as if her heart would break—not because the grave was occupied, but because it was empty. She had come prepared to anoint a dead body, but the body was not there at all. The stone rolled away could only mean that someone had stolen that beloved form. She had been doubly robbed—robbed in His death and robbed of a last opportunity to minister to Him and stay the cancer of corruption. John does not notice the other women accompanying Mary. It would seem from her words to the disciples about the unknown plunderers that others had been with her (v. 2), but John has thought only for the friendless Mary. Peter and John—having satisfied themselves that the graveclothes bore eloquent testimony, not of a hurried removal, but of an unhurried rising— went away home. Mary, however, remained to weep. What was home to one so terribly bereft of the light of her life!

Have we not stood there, too, when all that we held dear had gone? Death the enemy had robbed us and left us sad and lonely. If Jesus our Lord had not risen, we might well weep. What guarantee would we have that we shall not end in the grave, too? None at all. If death has dominion over Him, where shall the ungodly and the sinner appear?

In her grief, Mary stooped and looked again into the darkened tomb. Startled, she saw two angels in white sitting, one at the head and the other at the foot of the undisturbed graveclothes. It was as if they were covering the mercy seat of old (Ex. 37:8). The other evangelists record that the angels witnessed to the resurrection; John simply states that Mary saw them and turned away. What were angels to one who had lost her Beloved!

It was like our Lord to reward her with a sight of Himself, though she mistook Him for the gardener. *"Now in the place where Jesus was crucified there was a garden; and in the garden a new sepulcher, wherein was never man yet laid"* (Jn. 19:41). Jesus died and was buried in a garden. Not a cemetery, but a garden. Mary supposed the stranger to be the gardener, the one who buried dry-looking seeds and dead-looking bulbs and went away in the sure and certain hope of a resurrection—the one who watched and waited and weeded until things burst forth and grew, blossomed and beautified.

But was she far wrong? Has He not turned every cemetery into a garden for those who love Him? Do we not sow things, now that He is alive, rather than bury them? Do not let us make the mistake of supposing that we go to the graveyard to "bury our dead out of our sight." No, we go to a sowing, a sowing in a garden.

It is sown in corruption; it is raised in incorruption: It is sown in dishonor; it is raised in glory: it is sown in weakness; it is raised in power: It is sown a natural body; it is raised a spiritual body (1 Cor. 15:42-44).

Suppose Him to be the gardener after you have sown that dear body—that husband, that wife, that son, that daughter—and all is well. Shall He who marks where the sparrow falls, not know? Shall He not watch and wait for the rising again? The resurrection means that He will come into His garden and see to the plantings and the raisings. Oh, to hear His call, *"I am come into My garden, My sister, My spouse"* (Song 5:1), and to share in the glory of His rising!

Fearfulness: To the fearful disciples, gathered in the upper room, having the doors "fastened," as the word means, Jesus showed His hands and His side. Luke notices that our Lord showed His hands and feet; John, His hands and side. His hands of power, His side of pity.

The hands and the heart of Christ are for His own fearful ones. His hands to provide, His heart to care. The rich of earth have hands that could provide for our need, but they have no heart to do so. Our well-meaning friends have hearts to sympathize, but not the means to supply our need. In the resurrection, blessed be His Name, our Lord has both.

Are we afraid? Do our sins like a mountain tower above us, or like a heavy burden, are they too heavy for us? Then let His pierced hands and side speak peace to us. He was wounded for our transgressions, He was bruised for our iniquities. De we have no fear for eternal issues, but strangely enough, harbor fears about present possible eventualities? Fear of ill health, unemployment, bereavement, loneliness? These specters haunt us and disturb our rest.

The risen Christ is the cure. He would show us afresh His hands and side. None shall pluck us out of His hands. These powerful hands can hold and help and heal. His heart is touched with the feeling of our infirmities. *"We have not an high priest who cannot sympathize"* (Heb. 4:14, RV). "The heart of the Eternal is most wonderfully kind." *"Is not the life more than meat and the body than raiment?"* (Mt. 6:25) Will He who has given the life—the eternal things—not see to the food and the raiment? We betray the anomalous position of a people who, having no fear of our future transportation to heaven and of an amazing transformation even while we journey there, yet have fears of our daily sustenance while we wait for this glorious redemption.

In Luke 10 the Spirit of God has placed side by side the parable of the Good Samaritan and the account of Martha and Mary at the supper. In the former we read that the Samaritan "took care" of the rescued man at the inn. The sevenfold ministry of the Samaritan indicates the tender and perfect care for the unfortunate man. When the benefactor departed he gave money to the host of the inn for the man's future need. *"Take care of him,"* he said, *"and whatsoever more you spend, when I come again I will repay thee"* (Lk. 10:35). It is a picture of the unceasing care of our Saviour, and of His Church, to whom has been committed gifts *"for the perfecting of the saints, for the work of the ministry, for the edifying of the body of Christ"* (Eph. 4:12).

Alongside of this, Martha says, *"Lord, dost Thou not care that my sister hath left me to serve alone?"* (Lk. 10:40). Martha was concerned about the meal; Mary about the Master. Mary felt it was more important to hear His words than to leave Him alone while they both strove to get a meal adequate for the heavenly Guest. Did He not say that man does not live by bread alone, but by every word that proceeded out of the mouth of God? Martha was busy about things for the body, and was *"careful and troubled"* in doing so. These are the things that make us fearful and fretful. We do not doubt for a moment that, defying the laws of gravity, we shall be caught up to meet the Lord in the air; but we fear we may in the meantime be left to die of starvation. How often, however unspoken, the words are in our hearts, *"Lord, dost Thou not care...?"*

Let us allow Him to show us afresh His hands and side. *"Then were the disciples glad when they saw the Lord"* (Jn. 20:20). Sent forth with His message of peace, as we have seen, we must always keep His pierced, providing hands in view, and that pierced, pitying heart. *"My God shall supply all your need"* (Php. 4:19). The Philippians had once and again sent to the necessity of Paul. Their hearts and hands had been deeply affected by His hands and side. Paul would assure them that the divine heart appreciates this and divine hands would supply their own need from His infinite resources.

Faithlessness: Thomas was a twin, as *"Didymus"* indicates. We do not know about his twin, but he is easy to find, after all. He is like Thomas in his pessimism (Jn. 11:16), in his lack of perception (Jn. 14:5), in his peevishness and petulance (Jn. 20:25). He is like him in his absence, his argument, and, thank God, in his adoration.

ABSENCE: *"Thomas was not with them when Jesus came."* How much he lost by his absence from the assembly of disciples. They were given a faith-strengthening visit by the Lord; Thomas lingered and so languished in unbelief for another week. They were made glad by the sight; Thomas went on in despair.

How much we lose by our absence from the meetings of the saints, when our Lord often draws near and makes Himself known. He is often *"made known in the breaking of bread"* (Lk. 24:35). He is in the midst when two or three draw near in prayer (Mt. 18:20). He joins in the praise of the gathered Church (Ps. 22:22). But when we forsake the assembling of ourselves together, we miss these glorious manifestations, and are the poorer for it. Thomas' twin stays away from the meetings and wonders why he is not happy, why he has no strength to overcome.

ARGUMENT: *"Except I shall see in His hands the print of the nails, and put my finger into the print of the nails, and thrust my hand into His side, I will not believe"* (Jn. 20:25). Thomas' twin is not only absent from the assembled disciples; he ignores the testimony of those who claim to have seen the Lord. Thomas virtually charged his fellow disciples with an amazing credulity or with downright deception. He brushed aside the testimony of credible witnesses, and said harshly, adamantly, *"Except I shall see...I will not believe."*

The heroes of faith in Hebrews 11 endured as seeing Him who is invisible. By faith Abraham saw a city whose builder and maker was God. Believing is seeing. But Thomas' twin ignores those brethren or those books which would take away unbelief. By his dictum he would not believe any fact of history, however well it was authenticated. By it he would believe in neither Julius Caesar nor Jesus Christ. His aphorism displaces testimony and discounts Christian evidences.

ADORATION: *"And Thomas answered and said unto Him, My Lord and my God"* (Jn. 20:28). How gracious our Lord was with Thomas when, a week later, He again visited the upper room when the skeptical disciple was present. Jesus invited him to do what he declared was essential to faith. Yet we do not read that Thomas did put forth his hand and touch the fresh wounds of his Lord. The sight was enough and brought from his lips the confession of Christ's deity and His lordship; in fact, a confession of his personal acceptance of both. He is a type of those who, at the end of the age of the unbelief of Israel, will look upon Him whom they pierced.

> *And it shall be said in that day, Lo, this is our God; we have waited for Him, and He will save us: this is the Lord; we have waited for Him, we will be glad and rejoice in His salvation* (Isa. 25:9).

Note the close resemblance between the cry of Thomas and the cry of the people when *"the Lord of hosts shall reign in mount Zion, and in Jerusalem, and before His ancients gloriously"* (Isa. 24:23). Paul, too, appears to be the prototype of those who will confess Him Lord when they see Him. We hear him say,

> *This is a faithful saying, and worthy of all acceptation, that Christ Jesus came into the world to save sinners; of whom I am chief [first]. Howbeit...I obtained mercy, that in me first Jesus Christ might show forth all longsuffering, for a pattern to them which should hereafter believe on Him to life everlasting* (1 Tim. 1:15-16).

Paul viewed himself as one born prematurely (1 Cor. 15:8). He had seen Jesus the Lord (1 Cor. 9:1). He became not only a pattern to those who would come into Christ after him in the present age of the Church, but to those who after this age would believe on Him at the sight of Christ.

When Paul said he was the chief of sinners it may have been the candid confession of one who realized that one in the place of light and privilege has the greater responsibility and the greater condemnation if he fails to walk in that light. Sir Robert Anderson believed Paul was uttering sober truth. On the other hand it may have been the contrite cry of a truly holy man who realizes how far he comes short of the divine standard. He who said, *"I am the least of the apostles"* (1 Cor. 15:9), later wrote, *"I am less than the least of all saints"* (Eph. 3:8). Later still he writes that he is the *"chief of sinners."*

The third possibility is that Paul is the first of those who will be converted at the sight of the glorified Christ. They shall look upon Him whom they have pierced (Zech. 12:10). *"And one shall say unto Him, What are these wounds in Thine hands? Then He shall answer, Those with which I was wounded in the house of My friends"* (Zech. 13:6). Paul did not afterwards, as we have noted, rescind the confession of Lordship which sprang involuntarily at first to his lips when he heard the divine voice from heaven on the Damascus road. The identity of the speaker was not at first revealed. But when it was, the lordship of "Jesus" was owned by the persecutor. In the same way the identity of the resurrected Christ brought forth the great confession from Thomas. This is the confession which results in our salvation (Rom. 10:9), in our new birth (1 Jn. 5:1), in our calling to eternal life (1 Tim. 6:12).

These human frailties of friendlessness, fearfulness, and faithlessness, as we have said, remain with us today.

Only the risen Christ can cure them. Tears must go, for He makes every cemetery a garden for His own. Fears must go, for He brings the strength of His hands and the sympathy of His side. Unbelief must go and a glorious confession of faith take its place: *"Blessed are they that have not seen, and yet have believed"* (Jn. 20:29).

> *There may be days of darkness and distress,*
> *When sin has power to tempt, and care to press,*
> *Yet in the darkest day I will not fear,*
> *For, 'mid the shadows, Thou wilt still be near.*
>
> —H. L. R. DECK

FIVE

After These Things

After these things Jesus showed Himself again to the
disciples at the sea of Tiberias.
JOHN 21:1

In this chapter a closer look will show that we have a
record not merely of historical events which follow those
described in our last chapter, but of things which will
happen after the present age has run its course. If John
20 gives us the distinctive characteristics of the present
period, the closing chapter of his book gives us a
glimpse of what shall be *"after these things."* The ministry of our Lord on the shore may well remind us of our
meeting with Him *"on the other side,"* of the appraisal
of our service, and of the glad feast that will follow.

"Jesus showed Himself again." We seem to see in the
words a revelation of the Saviour's grace, of His glory,
and of His guidance. His grace is seen in being willing
to show Himself again to those who forsook Him and

fled. His glory is suggested in the catching and the counting of the fish and in the credit imputed to the disciples for the catch. When they reach the shore His guidance is needed, whether in the evangelical business of the fish or the pastoral care of the flock. Later the shepherds discover they are but sheep themselves, and are seen following the Great Shepherd. It is to these things we would first turn.

A revelation of grace: After the faithlessness and fearfulness of chapter 20, and that in spite of all that our Lord had said to them of His approaching death and resurrection, Jesus showed Himself again to His disciples. The names of some of the seven are given.

Peter is mentioned. After the carelessness of Peter in standing at the world's fire to warm himself, after the carnal confidence of Peter in stating that though all should be offended in Jesus he would not, after the cowardice and the cursing of Peter, Jesus showed Himself to him. *"Go, tell the disciples and Peter"* (Mk. 16:7).

Thomas is mentioned. After the unbelief of Thomas, after his absence and his argument, after his pessimism and deplorable lack of perception, Jesus showed Himself to him.

Nathaniel is mentioned. He comes before us in the first chapter of John's Gospel. Our Lord called him an Israelite in whom was no guile—no "Jacob." *"Because,"* said He, *"I said I saw thee under the fig tree, believest thou? Thou shalt see greater things than these"* (Jn. 1:50). Nathaniel had seen these greater things—yet, after seeing them, had joined with those who forsook their Master and fled under the pressure of the opposition. These greater things are doubtless embodied in this Gospel—wondrous grace to the guileless but apparently timid Nathaniel.

The sons of Zebedee are mentioned. John himself, one of them, does not designate himself here, as usual in his Gospel, *"the disciple whom Jesus loved."* Perhaps he felt, in narrating the event years after, that in the night of failure that followed this desire to go fishing, he did not merit the beloved appellation. But John and James, unnamed but distinguishable, are there—the ambitious, the ardent (see Mk. 10:35-39; Lk. 9:54).

Two others are there, but not distinguishable, making seven in all—the perfect number but imperfect men. They represent the whole Church, as we shall see, composed of men of different characteristics. We have our aggressive Peters, our argumentative Thomases, our artless Nathaniels, our ardent Johns and Jameses, as well as that unnamed, unknown host, symbolized by the two at the end of the list. To all these, grown tired of waiting for Him, Jesus shows Himself again.

Should we not take courage from this? Is not this same grace extended to us? After our carelessness and cowardice, after our peevishness and petulance, our inordinate ambition, can we not hope and pray that our Lord will show Himself again to us? *"He hath not dealt with us after our sins, nor rewarded us according to our iniquities." "If we believe not, He abideth faithful." "The gifts and calling of God are without repentance."*

A revelation of glory: Here is more than a hint indeed of the prophetic events after the things of the present age. After *"the things which are"* of Revelation 2 and 3, the present period of the churches, we have the third division of the book of Revelation, *"the things which shall be after these things"* (Rev. 1:19; 4:1). These things begin with the shout which ushers John (and the Church) into the glory. Here in John 21, all seven meet the Lord, though not in the same way. Peter leaves the others, and goes through the water to meet Him; the other six go over the water to their Lord. But all seven, with all their failings and failures, are united with Christ when the night is over.

None shall be lost on the way. The complete number which starts out reaches the shore where Christ is. The very figures of the Church in the New Testament forbid the idea of a "partial rapture," where only those found faithful or watching shall be caught up to meet the Lord. The Church is a body and a bride. The body shall be complete when the Head comes. The Bridegroom comes for the bride, not for part of her. The larger percentage of the Church has already gone through the waters of death. Whether carnal or spiritual, the bulk of the Church is at home with the Lord, for to be absent from the body is to be present with the Lord (2 Cor. 5:8). This being so, the remnant left on earth awaiting the shout of Christ shall not be divided. We who are living may go all together one of these days. Blessed prospect! Whether we go through or over the water, is of small moment. *"Whether we live or die, we are the Lord's"* (Rom. 14:8).

We shall bring our catch with us, and a proper count will be made.

Bring of the fish which ye have now caught. Simon Peter went up, and drew the net to land full of great fishes, a hundred and fifty and three: and for all there were so many, yet was not the net broken (Jn. 21:10-11).

How badly we count our catches today. We see cartoons and hear jokes about the exaggeration of earthly catches of fish, and we all know about the bigger ones that got away. This exaggeration is often reflected in the evangelist's account of his labors. He feels that his reputation is at stake, and he must bolster the number of his converts by counting the hands raised at his meetings. The net broke on an earlier occasion when Peter made but a halfhearted obedience to the Master's call to let down the net for a catch (Lk. 5:5-7). But here there is no failure. The net does not break though filled with the great fish, and the count is exact. None is lost.

How gracious of the Lord to reckon the catch as theirs. *"Bring of the fish which ye have now caught."* He gives them credit, as if the effort and the success were entirely their own. When we get to the Lord with our catch, He will do the same and then each shall have his praise of God.

In what follows we see in the interrogation of Peter a shadow of the judgment seat of Christ, when we shall give account of the deeds done in the body. Then we shall see our service in the true light, whether done for love to Christ or for love of self. *"Simon, son of Jonas, lovest thou Me more than these?"* By a *"fire of coals"* Jesus spoke to Peter. By a fire of coals Peter had warmed himself before and denied his Lord (Jn. 18:18). Peter had declared that though all the other disciples should be offended, yet he would not. He felt his was a deeper devotion, a greater courage. He loved his Master more than these, his fellows. Here by the fire Jesus reminded him of that confident assertion and of that recent and remorseful failure. Had his conduct proved his claim?

Then, too, all around Peter were the fatal attractions of the old life, from which he had been called away to become a fisher of men. Evidently growing tired of waiting for the risen Christ and the appointment in Galilee, Peter had gone fishing (Mt. 28:16). The boat, the nets, the glittering heap of fish, still drew Peter. Did he love the Lord more than these? His trip last night might have been pardonable, but was it profitable? Was love to Christ, whom he had been called to follow, the constraining motive of that expedition? In the first phase of Peter's testing, our Lord questioned the superiority of his love; in the second, the very existence of it, and in the third the very existence of the "affection" that Peter had asserted from the start. This last grieved the heart of Peter.

And love must be our constraining motive, too. The love of Christ constrains us. Without it, the most eloquent tongue, the most daring exploits, the most costly gifts, the most exquisite pains for the faith, are as nothing, as 1 Corinthians 13 shows us.

Joab was a great general. Under him David's kingdom

was extended and consolidated. But love for his master was not the constraining motive. David declared that Joab had often troubled him, and in the list of the mighty men of David he is absent. His name is actually mentioned three times in the list, but only to identify other men with whom he was associated. He himself has no honor. How much of our boasted service may be discounted in that day. How much of self goes into our work—far more than we realize. We are not building with pure gold, pure silver, precious stones. Our materials are alloyed with our own desires, our own glory, our own reward.

Note also in this chapter that Peter knew that he would live to be an old man (Jn. 21:15). Verse 19 may be John's commentary on the event after Peter's death had become history. Peter may not have apprehended his death at first. He certainly, however, had it before him when he wrote his second epistle. *"I will endeavor…that ye may be able after my decease [exodus] to have these things always in remembrance"* (2 Pet. 1:14-15). He who had seen or heard that earnest conversation going on between Moses and Elijah about the Lord's decease (exodus), which He should accomplish at Jerusalem, knew that he himself was not being borne to a place from which no traveler returned, but would be carried on through death to a glorious freedom of which Israel's exodus was but a type. It was all to be the result of that accomplishment of the Lord Jesus Christ.

Peter knew then that he would not remain until the Lord returned, though the possibility of John's continuance was not denied. *"If I will that he tarry till I come, what is that to thee?"* In view of this, any assertion that the Church could look any day after Pentecost for the return of Christ is not sustained. It is when Peter is conceivably *"old"* that Paul gives the *"word from the Lord"* (1 Thess. 4:15) in which the blessed hope is clarified. The dead in Christ shall not fail to participate in the glory of the return. They shall rise first. Then those who indeed tarry till He comes, shall be caught up with those thus raised, to meet the Lord in the air. This last chapter of John gives us a glimpse of that coming glory.

A revelation of guidance: In this chapter the metaphors of our ministry change quickly. First we have fishermen catching fish; then it is shepherds feeding sheep. Then the shepherds are but sheep themselves, needing to follow the Great Shepherd. Peter saw John following the Lord and was bidden to do the same.

There may be a hint of the work of the evangelist, the pastor, and the teacher, the three remaining gifts in the Church today, for the work of the ministry for the perfecting of the saints for the edifying of the Body of Christ. The evangelist catches the fish, the pastor feeds the lambs and the sheep, the teacher must ever follow the Lord closely, whether in death or life, as seen in Peter and John. Sometimes the ordeal of living for Christ is greater than the ordeal of dying for Him.

All need the guidance of the risen Lord on the shore. Evangelists do, as witness the unfruitful night on the lake. Perhaps the natural characteristics of these fishermen would guide us as to the cause of our unfruitful fishing. The impulsiveness of a Peter, the unbelief of a Thomas, the ambition and fleshly ardor of a James and a John, are among these causes of failure. We ask for souls and ask amiss, that we might consume our success upon ourselves. If we can just announce so many saved as a result of our preaching, people will know we are on the job and our services as evangelists worth securing. We pride ourselves that we have a reputation for success, and impulsively accept the invitations that come to us as the result of our own announced blessing elsewhere, with the result that the Lord can do no mighty work because of our selfishness and superficiality.

How much we need to remember, in the language of our chapter, that *"it is the Lord."* The disciple whom Jesus loved recognized His work. Who else could it be? Who else could give such a multitude of fishes a little more than a hundred yards from the shore? Their impetuous labor and zeal in the deep had produced nothing. Now at the right side and at the right moment, they had a great catch. It was the Lord's doing and marvelous in their eyes.

Here is guidance indeed for fishermen, our first lesson in the art of catching men. Paul might plant, Apollos water, but God gives the increase. The earnestness of a Paul, the eloquence of an Apollos, produce nothing in themselves. Of His own will He begets, by the Word of truth. Belief of the truth can result only from sanctification of the Spirit (2 Thess. 2:13). The Spirit of God must first brood over the face of the waters before God says,

"Let there be light." Souls that are really won for the Lord are *"elect according to the foreknowledge of God the Father, through sanctification of the Spirit, unto obedience and sprinkling of the blood of Jesus Christ"* (1 Pet. 1:2). It is a great thing to remember this. An evangelist's tears may be a sacred thing to behold, and he is but following in a sacred succession when he weeps, but his zeal must not consume him. It is the Lord. The success is His, though He may give us credit for the catch, as He did long ago by the lake.

Records of God-sent revivals will reveal times when sermons were read by shortsighted preachers who, holding their manuscript close to their eyes, were unaware of the convulsions of feeling going on in the congregations. It is the Lord. Let us acknowledge it. It is the primary lesson for all soul winners. The other lessons flow from it. These were good fishermen. They knew the lake and presumably had good equipment. They knew how advantageous it was to fish by night. Yet they caught nothing. Their curt reply to His call reflects their disappointment. But His command and direction changed everything. He knew where the fish were. The sea is His; He made it. The result of His guidance was a catch they had probably never seen—great fish and all counted. The significance of the number eludes us, as does the full significance of any catch for Christ. We shall know it only when we are on the shore with our Lord.

Guidance, too, in the care of the flock, may be indicated here. Those caught in the net for the Lord become sheep in a flock afterwards. They need tending. A glance at the words translated *"feed"* in John 21:15-17, will show that the feeding of the lambs and the sheep are first and last, while the "tending"—the ruling, the disciplining—are in the middle. This would suggest that the feeding is paramount. Where there is rich pasture the flock will flourish, and discipline will be the incidental thing. Mephibosheth was lame through careless nursing. The lambs are often berated for their wandering, but it may be the result of our poor feeding. They are not satisfied at home and go elsewhere for food. Feeding lambs is not as easy as we imagine. A preacher will often excuse himself for his lack of preparation by suggesting that what he has will do for the young in Christ, whereas such feeding calls for most careful and consecrated efforts.

In the three recorded incidents of our Lord's raising the dead, it is interesting to see the immediate activities of the persons raised. Jairus' daughter, youngest of all and who had just died, was lifted by the hand and given something to eat. The young man of Nain, evidently older than the girl and on the way to burial, was raised and began to speak. Lazarus, the oldest and dead four days, was called out of the tomb, loosed, and let go. The young children need something to eat; the *"young men"* need to have their mouths opened; the older ones know Him who is from the beginning (see 1 Jn. 2:12-14). They are to go for God.

Older sheep need to be fed, too. A poet has reminded us that it was a sheep, not a lamb, that went astray in the parable Jesus taught, and that if the sheep go wrong it will not be long before the lambs are as bad as they. That is of course true, and sheep of Christ's flock seem as they grow older to have less concern to feed themselves. So they must be fed by the shepherds. This ministry is enjoined, both by Paul and Peter, upon the elders who are addressed as overseers and bidden to feed the flock of God (Acts 20:17, 28; 1 Pet. 5:1-4). Peter reminds his readers that their service was before the eye of the Chief Shepherd who would reward them when He appeared.

This "feeding" calls for concentration and consecration on the part of all shepherds. We must *"look well to the state of the flocks"* (Prov. 27:23). Jacob was a good shepherd, watching night and day, in heat and in frost, over the flock (Gen. 31:40). Yet he could not say with the Good Shepherd that *"none of them is lost"* (Jn. 17:12).

Paul was a good shepherd, laboring and warning night and day, with tears (Acts 20:31; 1 Thess. 2:9). Such shepherds find that feeding the flock is first and last in the care of the flock. Their "ruling" will not be as lords over God's heritage, but as guides and examples to the flock. They will restore in a spirit of meekness those that are overtaken in a trespass (Gal. 6:1). The need for a sterner discipline in individual cases often results from the general condition of the flock.

The need for a solemn act of excommunication should be a fresh occasion for shepherds to be before the Lord in confession of failure and for food *"convenient"*— suitable—for the sheep. Surely our Lord here, in the glory of His rising, would guide us throughout this age.

Guidance for the shepherds in their personal lives is in

the chapter, too, for they themselves are but sheep needing to follow their Master. *"Peter, turning about, seeth the disciple whom Jesus loved following...Jesus saith unto him...follow thou Me."* In the beginning of this Gospel two disciples of John the Baptist follow Jesus. John, the writer of this Gospel, may have been one of them. If so, he is still following at the end. We can only follow Paul as he followed Christ (1 Cor. 11:1).

Disciples who the day before beheld the Lamb of God as One who had come to take away the sin of the world, now look *"upon Jesus as He walked"* (Jn. 1:36). His walking and talking were always in perfect suitability. Luke's first treatise was of all that Jesus began both to *do* and to *teach.* His doing was always in harmony with His teaching. The bell was always followed by a pomegranate on the hem of His garment round about (Ex. 39:26).

Those shepherds of the flock who are themselves following Jesus will ever seek the holy harmony of life and lip. Like their Master, they will speak with authority and not as the scribes. They will emulate Him in His fervency, His faithfulness, His fearlessness. They will search the records of His commands to see if they are observing *"whatsoever He hath commanded"* (Mt. 28:20). They will seek out the terms of the great commission afresh to see if they faithfully carry it out. They will realize that the commands of the apostles are no less the commands of Christ (2 Pet. 3:1-2).

John shows us in his Gospel the Master Evangelist at work, the Master Fisher of men, in drawing individuals into His net. He portrays the Good Shepherd who gave

His life for the sheep, and portrays the Teacher come from God (Jn. 3:2). The glory of His rising is that He has given such gifts to the Church, and the power to become fervent evangelists, faithful pastors, and fearless teachers. He serves best who knows he is but a follower himself, needing the care of the Shepherd and Bishop of his soul (1 Pet. 2:25).

The WITNESS of LUKE

The Message to the World

SIX

Divine Openings

Their eyes were opened and they knew Him...
He opened unto them the Scriptures...
then opened He their understanding.
LUKE 24:31, 32, 45

Luke, the Gentile writer of the third Gospel, as we have noted, is more concerned with the witness of the resurrection in and around Jerusalem, as Matthew the Jew is with hurrying on to the testimony in Galilee. Luke's account bears the graphic character of an eyewitness. He desires to show by his Grecian or Hellenistic witness Cleopas, that the facts and glories of resurrection are not for Jews only, but for *"all nations"* (Lk.24:47). He desires to emphasize, above all else, the importance of the holy Scriptures as a material witness, indeed Exhibit One, of the resurrection. It was according to the things written aforetime that *"repentance and remission of sins should be preached in His name among all nations"* (Lk. 24:47). There was not simply Hebrew but Hellenistic witness.

Luke notices too, that the women came in considerable numbers to the sepulcher, that they received the news of the rising again of Jesus, but does not record that the Lord appeared to them. He follows his associate Paul in leaving out the appearances of our Lord to women (1 Cor. 15:5-8), but he contrasts sharply the devotion and faith of these females with the unbelief and slowness of heart of the males. Paul leaves out the Emmaus revelations, while Luke enlarges upon them. It is to these Lucan insertions that we draw attention.

Instead of coming to an end in chapter 24 as we might suppose, we find that Luke's Gospel has been a grand introduction to a wonderful story contained in the physician's second book, the Acts of the Apostles. The account goes on through the present age, and will be consummated only when the last work of faith and labor of love has been recorded. The *"former treatise"* of Luke contains what Jesus began both to do and teach (Acts 1:1). The Acts is the story of what He continued to do from heaven and through the Holy Spirit. These divine openings at the end of the Gospel furnish us with the results of that life and death so warmly portrayed by the beloved physician, and which created the glorious evangel in all the world as recorded in the Acts.

The chapter begins with the open grave at the opening of the week. This is followed by the opened Scriptures, expounded by the risen Lord to the two Emmaus disciples. The home opened to the Stranger, who had so warmed the hearts of these disappointed disciples, results in the eyes of the owners being opened to know the Lord. Later, among the eleven and those with them, the understanding of these tardy believers was opened to comprehend the Scriptures. Later still, after heaven opened—the everlasting doors to receive the King of Glory (Ps. 24:7-8)—the disciples returned to Jerusalem with great joy, and were continually in the temple praising and blessing God. Their mouths were opened.

Luke's Gospel begins with a dumb priest in the temple, because he believed not the angel's words; it closes with the priests of a coming new order, in the temple court with mouths open to praise God. These are *"divine openings"* and demand a closer look.

The opened grave: It looks indeed as if Joseph, the rich man of Arimathea, had been preparing a long time beforehand for the burial of Jesus. Perhaps we should think of this devoted follower as acquainted with the prophetic Scriptures that spoke of men making Christ's grave with the wicked, but being with the rich in His death, because He had done no violence (Isa. 53:9). Perhaps the grave had been purchased some time before, adjacent to the place of the skull where transgressors habitually died, so that when the time came for His numbering among them, everything would be ready. Joseph was waiting for the moment when death would take place, and he would seek permission to bear away the precious body of the Lord and be the instrument in fulfilling the words of Isaiah. The women who came from Galilee evidently followed Joseph, and observed the place and manner of His burial, after which they went home to purchase and prepare spices, to come to anoint our Lord's body after the rest of the Sabbath, early on the first day of the week.

The assertion of Renan that some "hysterical women" came to the grave, hoping in their hearts that Jesus was risen and were therefore prepared to "see things" in the gray light of the morning, is foolish in light of the artless account. Nothing could be further from the truth. See what they bear in their hands—spices to anoint a dead body! Hear what they say as they approach: *"Who shall roll us away the stone?"* They were not triumphant at finding the stone rolled away and the body gone, but perplexed and fearful and amazed. The body was gone and angels said Jesus was raised. Why seek the living among the dead?

The grave was indeed open. The Lord was risen indeed. The rage and scorn of His enemies could not produce a corrupting body to put an end to the Christian movement, nor could they induce His friends to produce it. They will die for their faith. They will never, under the extreme cruelty of their death, break down and confess fraud. Thereby He is *"declared the Son of God with power...by the resurrection from the dead"* (Rom. 1:4). Thereby His words are fulfilled and His claims vindicated. *"Destroy this temple, and in three days I will raise it up." "The Son of Man shall be betrayed into the hands of men, and they shall kill Him, and the third day He shall be raised again"* (Mt. 27:22-23). *"I, if I be lifted up from the earth, will draw all men unto Me."* Thereby is demonstrated Christ's ability to save His people to the uttermost, and His fitness to judge the world in righteousness (Acts 17:31; Heb. 7:25; Lk. 24:7; Jn. 2:19; Jn. 12:32). Thereby, too, our inheritance in heaven is reserved for us, and we reserved for it (1 Pet. 1:3-4).

The open grave stands at the start of the week in this chapter, as it stands at the dawn of days for all of us who have put our trust in our Lord. Men stand with bowed heads at the graves of their heroes; the Christian utters a glad hallelujah at the empty tomb of his Lord. The writer never forgets the thrill of looking into the tomb of President George Washington at Mount Vernon, to see in the glow of a strong light the words: "*I am the resurrection and the life: he that believeth in Me, though he were dead, yet shall he live"* (Jn. 11:25). It was a declaration of the faith of the first president of the United States. His body was in the grave, but the open grave of Jesus assured him, as it assures men of like faith, that he shall rise.

The opened Scriptures: *"He opened unto [them] the Scriptures."* Luke desires to show that the sufferings of Christ were to be expected on the basis of the prophecies that went before. The leaders of Israel greatly erred, *"not knowing the Scriptures."* The disciples failed for the same reason (Jn. 20:9). Note the frequent references to these sacred writings and to the words of Jesus in this chapter before us. His *"words" "the prophets," "Moses* *and all the prophets," "the Scriptures," "the Psalms" "thus it is written."* With Paul, Luke's exhibit A in the evidence is the sacred Word. There is nothing as powerful as the holy Scriptures to move us for God. True missionary motivation is not the result of emotional missionary appeal, but of the command of the Lord of the harvest. External Christian evidences have their place, but they can never take the place of scriptural witness. Regeneration can never be the result of clever arguments but of the grace and Spirit of God.

The two Emmaus disciples were evidently returning home to take up, as best they could, the threads of the old life. Luke is careful to tell us that one of the two was named Cleopas, a Gentile or an Hellenistic Jew.

Was the other himself? Luke wants us to know, as we have said, that the Greek-speaking world was represented in the first witnesses of the resurrection. The good news was for the whole world.

It was not simply that hope deferred had made the heart of these disciples sick. The hope was gone. *"We trusted that it had been He who should have redeemed Israel"* (Lk. 24:21). They spoke of their faith as in the past. How keenly must the Stranger have felt when He heard this sad declaration of an abortive faith. They had been unaware of Him at first as they "threw back" to one another, as the word used suggests, the enigma of the recent happenings at Jerusalem. There was nothing to do but return home and try to forget the crashing of their hopes and dreams. But life would never be the same. They walked and were sad.

The One who drew near in the gathering darkness may have listened for some time to the dispirited conversation before intruding Himself into it. *"What manner of communications are these that ye have one to another, as ye walk and are sad?"* To Cleopas it seems to come as a surprise, not the divine eavesdropping, but that anyone should be ignorant of the surpassing topic of their conversation. Surely there could only be one subject, concerning Jesus of Nazareth, a prophet mighty in deed and word before God and all the people. But He was dead and their hopes had died with Him, in spite of the vision and testimony of angels which certain women were supposed to have had, attesting that Jesus was alive.

It was at this point that Jesus broke in with the witness of the Word. Beginning at Moses and all the prophets, He expounded to them the things concerning the Christ. He ought, according to the Scriptures, not only to have suffered these things at Calvary, but to rise and enter into His glory.

What an unfolding of Scripture they had that evening, and from the Prince of Expositors Himself! Speaking of it afterwards, they said, *"Did not our heart burn within us, while He talked with us by the way, and while He opened to us the Scriptures?"* As Peter afterward saw the necessity for the *"sufferings of Christ"* and made them the central theme of his first epistle, so Luke, the writer of the Emmaus discourse, sees this supreme importance also and makes these sufferings prominent in the evangelism of the Acts. To Him give all the prophets witness.

Christ opened the Scriptures. We believe a careful

reading of the Old Testament discloses that, as Dr. Anstey has said, it is a book of unexplained ceremonies, of unfulfilled prophecies, and of unsatisfied longings. Its ceremonies are detailed and strange, but not explained as to their significance. The prophecies are numerous and diversified, but are not all fulfilled. The longings, among prophets and priests and kings, for a greater than themselves who would speak with greater authority and remain in office, are not satisfied when the Old Testament ends. The closing words of the volume are significant. *"Lest I...smite the earth with a curse"* (Mal. 4:6). The book ends disappointingly.

But the opening words of the New Testament lead us to hope for something better, and the Gospel stories which follow fulfill our expectation. We see that Jesus our Lord is the Great Explainer of the ceremonies, the Great Fulfiller of the prophecies, and the Great Satisfier of the longings. He is a prophet, the One whom Moses longed for and spoke of. *"The Lord thy God will raise up unto thee a Prophet...like unto me; unto Him ye shall hearken"* (Deut. 18:15). He is a priest after the order of Melchizedek (Ps. 110:4). He is a king, for to this end was He born. This second volume ends, not with a curse, but in a blessing. *"The grace of our Lord Jesus Christ be with you all"* (Rev. 22:21). We only have to compare the opening chapters of Genesis with the closing ones of Revelation to see how surely the strands of the one are woven into the web of the other.

Moreover, Old Testament characters become types of Him who was to come. Abel and Isaac and Joseph in

Genesis, Moses and Aaron in Exodus, Boaz in Ruth, David in 1 Samuel, Elisha in 2 Kings, Jonah and Daniel in the books that bear their names, do things which are repeated and enhanced by Jesus Christ our Lord. We see that the lives of these men are not recorded simply for ethical reasons, but for typical ones. They spoke of Him. Their accumulated witness proves that Jesus is the Christ. Those biographical foreshadowings, indicated in an earlier chapter, could be greatly enlarged. Christ opens the Scriptures. It is significant that these two Emmaus disciples must first get a course in prophetic Christology before the fact of resurrection is revealed to them. The Scriptures lead to the expectation. The sufferings and the glory to follow are clearly testified (see 1 Pet. 1:10-11).

Opened eyes: *"Their eyes were opened, and they knew Him"* (Lk. 24:31). All too soon the journey from Jerusalem to Emmaus, which had promised to be so long, came to an end. They were at their door before they were aware of it and the Stranger made as if He would go on into the night. But He must not be allowed to go. They must *"consider the heart of a stranger."* They would constrain Him, not simply for His sake, but for their own. His words were found and they did eat them, and they had become the joy and rejoicing of their heart. They asked Him into their home, and when they did, their eyes were opened. They were willing to open their doors to Him; He opened their eyes to know Him.

What a difference between the opened eyes of Genesis

3 and the opened eyes of Luke 24. *"And the eyes of both of them were opened, and they knew that they were naked." "And their eyes were opened, and they knew Him."* The first was the humiliating vision of themselves; the latter the heartening vision of the Lord. The first was to send the guilty pair into hiding; the second to send them away with the glad message of the Saviour's victory. Satan had promised opened eyes to that first pair, and the knowledge of good and evil, but all they got was a knowledge without power—without power either to do the good or to refuse the evil. It was left to Him who was to come, the virgin's Son, to know how *"to refuse the evil, and choose the good"* (Isa. 7:14-15).

Satan promises opened eyes to the sons of men. From the Gnosticism of the first century of the Christian era until the present-day cults, the reward of the devotees is to have knowledge, insight far beyond the possibility of a mere orthodox Christianity. We are told that when we really have our eyes opened, we shall perceive that there is no reality to sin at all, or to death and judgment. These are "errors of the mortal mind." While heaven might be a possibility, hell is impossible and absurd. Men who believe in this have not had their eyes opened. They are not the knowing ones. The pristine pair in the Garden of Eden at least knew that they were naked; these have no such knowledge and seek no covering.

But the heart opened to the Son of God has full knowledge. It knows Him. The knowledge of the Person of Jesus is not the result of the mere letter of theology, or of a mental acquiescence in divine things. Christian evidences show only the credibility of faith. The door which we open to the Son of God is not of the head, but of the heart, and when we do open it, we know Him. We might have known about Him before; now we know Him.

The change is not mental, or psychological; it is in the higher realm of the spirit. We are not concerned now with arguments for or against the Christian book, for or against the deity of Christ, or of immortality. We know Him, and in doing so our uncertainty about the other things vanishes We believe at once that His acts were miracles, and His words oracles. He speaks with authority to us. He has no doubt about the authority of the Scriptures, or His deity, or immortality, or creation. He asserts that God made man in the beginning. Man is not an evolution from lower forms of life. Such a view would be incompatible with the assertions of *"this teacher come from God,"* and of the Christian faith.

The writer was introduced to a man who had made a hobby of a knowledge of the Old Testament. He could tell with rare precision where any incident was found, and delighted many groups with his accurate answers to their questions. When we asked him if he were a Christian, he replied in the negative. He confessed to being an evolutionist and felt that was a fatal barrier to his being called a believer. We pointed out that the terms of being a child of God did not consist in not believing man originated from a slime pit, but in believing on our Lord Jesus Christ. The mighty, matchless text of the gospel, John 3:16, did not state that whosoever believeth in creation should not perish but have everlasting life, but whosoever believeth in Him, God's Son and God's gift. But we added immediately that a personal acceptance of God's Son would at once result in the man's believing in "the creation" spoken of by our Lord. The indwelling Spirit would bear witness at once to the truth of God. The opened door of the heart would result in the opened eyes.

The inner eyes of the erstwhile persecutor of the Church, Saul of Tarsus, were never more open than when he was *"three days without sight, and did neither eat nor drink."* The holy vision of Stephen, the heavenly vision of Jesus, was followed by the humbling vision of himself. His former life lay in shattered fragments at his feet. He was now a minister and a witness both of the things he had seen and of the things in which Christ would appear to him, delivering him from the people and the Gentiles, unto whom he was now sent, *"to open their eyes, and to turn them from darkness to light, and from the power of Satan unto God"* (Acts 26:16-18). Those with Paul saw the phenomenon of the light above the brightness of the sun, but heard not the voice that spoke to Saul. We can accept the miracles, the credentials of the Christian faith, without accepting the Christ.

While He is the Sovereign One who *"openeth and no man shutteth, and shutteth and no man openeth"* yet if any man hears His voice and opens the door, He will come in to him at once. It is then the eyes are opened to His Person, His beauty, His sufficiency.

Before leaving this section, let us note that after eating

with the two disciples, our Lord vanished out of their sight. Here we have not only a proof of the reality of resurrection, but a hint of the spiritual beauty and freedom of the new body for us all. The eating was not a necessity for the new body, but a proof of the physical resurrection. It had the power of eating, a body of flesh and bones.

Opened understanding: *"Then opened He their understanding, that they might understand the Scriptures"* To the two disciples on the road, Jesus expounded from Moses and the Prophets; here to the larger company He added the Psalms. There the sufferings of Christ are seen in the expiation of the sacrifices of old, and in the expectation of the seers. Here in the upper room, with the eleven and those gathered with them, we have the Psalms in which these sufferings are seen in the experience of the Psalmist. These experiences had been His, and in lesser degree would be theirs as they witnessed for Him. They, too, for His sake would be killed all the day long and be accounted as sheep for the slaughter (Rom. 8:36). Things concerning Himself thus equally pervade every part of Scripture and for these our Lord grants the opened understanding. In His absence today, the Spirit of God takes of the things of Christ, and shows them to us (Jn. 16:14-15)

We need this enlightenment. For this Paul prays on behalf of the Ephesians.

Wherefore I also, after I heard of your faith in the Lord Jesus, and love unto all the saints, cease not to give thanks for you, making mention of you in my prayers; that the God of our Lord Jesus Christ, the Father of glory, may give unto you the spirit of wisdom and revelation in the knowledge of Him: the eyes of your understanding being enlightened; that ye may know what is the hope of His calling, and what the riches of the glory of His inheritance in the saints, and what is the exceeding greatness of His power to us-ward who believe" (Eph. 1:15-19).

Again in Ephesians 3 the apostle prays for enlightenment, enduement, and enlarging in the broad sweep of the purposes of God and in the surpassing knowledge of the love of Christ. These blessings come, not to him who is clever, but to him who is consecrated; not to him who is wise after the flesh, but to him who is willing to do His will. *"If any man is willing to do His will, he shall know..."* (Jn. 7:17). We still need to come to Moses, to the prophets, and to the Psalms, with the prayer, *"Lord, open Thou mine eyes, that I may behold wondrous things out of Thy law"* (Ps. 119:18).

Opened mouths:

And it came to pass, while He blessed them, He was parted from them, and carried up into heaven. And they worshiped Him, and returned to Jerusalem with great joy: and were continually in the temple, praising and blessing God (Lk. 24:50-51).

Lift up your heads, O ye gates; and be ye lift up, ye everlasting doors; and the King of glory shall come in Who is this King of glory? The Lord strong and mighty, the Lord mighty in battle (Ps. 24:7-8).

The beloved physician seems anxious to see the "man child," whom he so warmly introduces at the beginning, caught up safely to heaven at the end (Rev. 12:5). If earthly doors are closed to Jesus, the everlasting doors of heaven are open. Reading Luke's account, we would imagine that the ascension of our Lord took place at the close of that first day of resurrection, whereas his account really covers the whole forty days of Christ's appearances. While our Lord could not be a priest on earth according to Jewish law, seeing He was not of the tribe of Levi, yet Luke shows Him in priestly scenes and would anticipate His heavenly priesthood. Whereas, as we have noted, there is at the beginning of his Gospel a priest who cannot bless because he is dumb, there is at the end One who can.

Moses blessed the people (Deut. 33:1), but his blessing was rather a dubious thing and he went up on high to die. Christ blessed His people indeed and went up on high to live for them. Moses, that man of vision, of vigor, and of virtue, as the closing chapters of Deuteronomy show, was dead. Another was needed, Joshua (the savior), to lead Israel into rest; but our Saviour lives and blesses His people. He shelters them by His atonement; He saves them by His advocacy.

And His people are priests, too, and their mouths are open, praising and blessing God. The temple heard such shouts of praise as it had not heard in many a year. The courts rang with them. As in the days of Nehemiah, when *"the joy of Jerusalem was heard even afar off,"* these men poured the new wine of their joy into the old wineskins of the temple. The skins would burst and vanish away in time. The Church of the living God would succeed the temple. The latter would soon close its doors to the followers of the Nazarene, but as yet the joyful worshippers thronged the courts. They must praise the Lord. They could do nothing less.

We must do the same. These divine openings cannot but fill our mouths with mirth and our hearts with joy. His praise must continually be on our lips. By Him we must offer the sacrifice of praise continually, the fruit of our lips, giving thanks to His Name. Christ is our Janus, the Opener of the doors. He has the keys, even of hell and of death (Rev. 1:18).

> *Praise the Saviour, ye who know Him;*
> *Who can tell how much we owe Him?*
> *Gladly let us render to Him*
> *All we are and have.*

What great discoveries this chapter contains! Let us notice them before we leave Luke's account. Jesus Himself from the grave; Jesus Himself in the Scriptures; Jesus Himself on the road, revealing Himself to the sad and the disappointed as He does today; Jesus Himself in the home, when we say, *"Abide with us: for it is toward evening, and the day is far spent"*; Jesus Himself in the Church, for where two or three are gathered together, even in an upper room, there He is in the midst; Jesus Himself in the glory—a real Man—our Forerunner and Representative. Aaron was a representative but not a forerunner. Christ, our divine Lord, not only appears in the presence of God for us, but announces our coming there also, and prepares a place for us, blessed be His Name. Then we shall have the greatest discovery of all, to see Him face to face, and to be like Him forever.

> *And is it so, I shall be like Thy Son?*
> *Is this the grace which He for me has won?*
> *Father of Glory (thought beyond all thought!)*
> *In glory, to His own blest likeness brought!*
>
> *Yet it must be; Thy love had not its rest*
> *Were Thy redeemed not with Thee fully blest,*
> *That love that gives not as the world, but shares*
> *All it possesses with its loved co-heirs.*
>
> —J. N. DARBY

The WITNESS of MATTHEW and MARK

The Message to Israel

SEVEN

The Sign
and the Signs Following

Attention has been drawn to the fact that Matthew seems to hurry on to the Galilean appearances of our Lord in resurrection. He seems to regard them, particularly the one by special appointment of Jesus, as the most important of all. He says nothing of the principal appearances in Jerusalem, as we might suppose, but simply states that the fear of some women was taken away by the words of the angel and later by our Lord's own words to them. The apostolic writers, Matthew and John, are concerned with the internal feelings of the witnesses, as Mark and Luke are with the outward circumstances of the resurrection itself. John, however, is interested in the interviews with individual characters, Matthew with the general outline of events.

The authority of the King is still seen in Matthew, in the glory of His rising. Both angels and nature are seen to serve Him, in bursting the bars by which men would seek to hinder His rising. The angel sat in solemn disdain upon the stone, emblem of the impotency of the Jews and of the Romans to hold Him. He would ignore alike the seal of the Jews and the soldiers of the Gentiles. The chief priests and Pharisees remembered, if Christ's disciples had not, that He said, *"After three days I will rise again." "Command,"* said they, *"that the sepulcher be made sure until the third day."*

Note the words, *"After three days"* and *"until the third day,"* in Matthew 27:63-64. They throw light on the problem of the time our Lord was in the grave, and seem to obviate the necessity of striving for a 72-hour period. (See Gen. 40:12, 20; Est. 4:16; 5:1). In each of these cases a full three days is not contemplated, a part of a day standing for the whole.

With authority from the Roman governor, the leaders of Israel sealed the stone at the mouth of the grave, and set a watch. The angel of the Lord came down from heaven to set aside the authority of men; and nature, as at His death, would by the great earthquake aid, if she could, the supremacy of heaven.

Kings of the earth set themselves, and the rulers take counsel together, against the Lord, and against His anointed, saying, Let us break their bands asunder, and cast away their cords from us (Ps. 2:2-3).

The council of governor and priests and Pharisees would make the cords and bands of His tomb "more sure," but they were blasted that Easter morning. It was not that the shattered emblem of authority was rolled away to let the Conqueror free: it was to bear witness that He was not there, but risen, as He said. The undisturbed graveclothes bore eloquent proof of it. The *"sign of the prophet Jonah"* was complete (Mt. 12:40).

Matthew is impressed with the sense of urgency in the resurrection message.

Go quickly, and tell His disciples that He is risen from the dead....And they departed quickly from the sepulcher with fear and great joy; and did run to bring His disciples word...Go tell My brethren that they go into Galilee, and there shall they see Me...Go ye therefore, and teach all nations (Mt. 28:7-8, 10, 19).

Note also the three references to Galilee. The "go" is to Galilee, and from there to the ends of the earth.

However, there must be an official and formal witness to Israel. If there is a band of messengers coming from the tomb in the mingled emotions of fear and great joy, there is another with fear and foreboding of judgment. The *"watch"* set by the Jews had become as dead men before the angel of the Lord. When some of them recovered, they rushed to the chief priests with the story of the heavenly visitor and of the empty grave.

What will these custodians of religion in Israel do? Will they bow to the testimony, not only of the soldiers, but of the Saviour Himself, and of the holy Scriptures? No, they will reject it.

And when they were assembled with the elders, and had taken counsel, they gave large money unto the soldiers, saying, Say ye, His disciples came by night, and stole Him away while we slept (Mt. 28:12-13).

Truly the rulers take counsel together against the Lord and against His Christ. They will corrupt the heathen soldiers who brought them the testimony, and with the most glaring falsification, discount it altogether. What cabal and blatant unbelief! These witnesses must be bribed to say that while they slept the disciples came and stole the body of Jesus. Sleeping men able to identify the thieves and divine their purpose! And the report is circulated and, as ever, finds many believers.

> *I was a Roman soldier in my prime;*
> *Now age is on me and the yoke of time.*
> *I saw the risen Christ, for I am he*
> *Who reached the hyssop to Him on the tree;*
> *And I am one of two who watched beside*
> *The sepulcher of Him we crucified.*
> *All that last night I watched with sleepless eyes:*
> *Great stars arose and crept across the skies.*
> *The world was all too still for mortal rest,*
> *For pitiless thoughts were busy in the breast.*
> *The night was long, so long, it seemed at last*
> *I had grown old and a long life had passed.*
> *Far off, the hills of Moab, touched with light*
> *Were swimming in the hollow of the night.*
> *I saw Jerusalem all wrapped in cloud,*
> *Stretched like a dead thing in a shroud.*
> *Once in the pauses of our whispered talk*
> *I heard a something on the garden walk.*

Perhaps it was a crisp leaf lightly stirred;
Perhaps it was the dream-note of a waking bird.
Then suddenly an angel burning white
Came down with earthquake in the breaking light;
And rolled the great stone from the sepulcher,
Mixing the morning with a scent of myrrh.
And lo, the Dead had risen with the day:
The Man of Mystery had gone His way!
Years have I wandered, carrying my shame;
Now let the truth of Time eat out my name.
For we, who all the wonder might have told,
Kept silence, for our mouths were stopt with gold!

Matthew, as His Master, will ignore the center of Judaism and go to Galilee of the Gentiles. He only notices the eleven going to Galilee as leaders of the larger company of followers. The some who doubted make you aware of the larger company. From there the King issues His commands.

> *Go ye therefore, and teach all nations, baptizing them in the name of the Father, and of the Son, and of the Holy Ghost: teaching them to observe all things whatsoever I have commanded you: and, lo, I am with you alway, even unto the end of the world* (Mt. 28:19-20).

The power and the presence were His; the program were theirs. The authority, as well as the enabling, would be to the end of the age. Their parish was all the world—all nations. The program was all the things He had commanded during His sojourn among them.

Note that the program did not end with what we sometimes call the "simple gospel." These disciples were not to be traveling preachers with the simple message of His death for sinners, but preachers traveling with the whole program of the Lord's teaching before them. Peter speaks of the commands of the Lord and Saviour through the apostles, which introduces us to the whole teaching of the New Testament. He, therefore, who claims a commission from Matthew 28 to go forth to preach to all nations, must abide by the terms of it—to teach New Testament doctrine, after having baptized his converts in the Name of the Triune God.

While the emphasis in Mark 16 is on the believer to be baptized, in Matthew 28 it is upon the preacher to baptize his converts and teach the commands of Christ. These commands, including the Sermon on the Mount, must not be relegated to Israel. We must not suppose that in some way they were better equipped to carry them out than we are, or that they will be in an age to come. There can be no higher equipment for character and conduct than we have in the present dispensation, with the indwelling Spirit of God in our hearts, the completed Word of God in our hands, and our ascended Lord as our unfailing High Priest and Advocate. Since, too, the entire sermon is seen in principle in the letters to the churches, we are bound to note the fourscore commands of our Saviour recorded in Matthew's Gospel and teach them. How can we teach whatsoever He has commanded if we ignore these precepts? Would there not be a return to apostolic power if there were a return to the whole terms of our commission as His missionaries? We should know His presence as He has promised, in a special way, even if we should run counter to the boards and committees of those at home.

Matthew leaves the King on the earth, while Mark takes Him to heaven. The King will yet reign on the earth, the knowledge of the Lord covering the earth as the waters cover the sea. He will be the true Son of Abraham (Mt. 1:1) for Abraham was heir of the world (Rom. 4:13). In Him shall all the families of the earth be blessed. What a day! His Name shall endure forever.

> *His Name shall be continued as long as the sun: and men shall be blessed in Him: all nations shall call Him blessed...Let the whole earth be filled with His glory. Amen, and Amen"* (Ps. 72:17-19).

THE WITNESS OF MARK

Mark's account is the shortest of all the evangelists. If we were to follow some of the older manuscripts we would omit verses 9-20 of chapter 16 altogether, and find that Mark had contented himself with the witness of the women who were early at the grave. It was like the Lord to reward these devoted women, who as soon as the Sabbath was past, went out and procured the spices to anoint the body of their Lord early the next morning. But the inclusion of the words from verse 9 to the end of the chapter seems to have the approval of most scholars, and the last verse seems a fitting climax to the purpose of Mark to portray the perfect Servant. The book opens, not with the helplessness of the baby in Bethlehem, but with the activity of the Servant of Jehovah who deals prudently always. The key word of Mark, occurring some forty times and translated *"immediately," "forthwith"* shows the devotion of the Son-Servant. Even when hid from the eyes of men in the glory, He still is seen working. *"And they went forth, and preached everywhere, the Lord working with them, and confirming the word with signs following"* (v. 20). No uninspired pen would have brought the Gospel to such a perfect end.

Taking the chapter as it stands, then, we see that while other women come into the foreground, our Lord first appears to Mary Magdalene, once dominated by demons. Wondrous grace! He did not appear to the disciples first, much less to the leaders of Israel or to Pilate—to confound them by His presence—but to Mary who loved much. Heaven's revelations are not usually to the learned, but to the lowly. Not many wise after the flesh are called.

Matthew and John, the Gospel writers from among the apostles, do not record the intention of the women to anoint a dead body, but Mark and Luke do. Nor do the apostolic writers record the unbelief of the men at the news the women brought, though they do not minimize their own unbelief at the appearances of Christ. Mark and Luke, however, state that the women had somewhat of their joy taken away by the unbelief of the men.

We notice here, too, the gradual increase of the witnesses, first one, then two, then eleven, with the summary suggesting a greater number present. The commission as given to them is like that of Matthew, with the different emphasis, as we have seen, on baptism. Mark, the imperfect servant, in whom Paul lost confidence for a time, but who is chosen now to write of the Perfect Servant, is anxious to show that the obedience of faith will include baptism. The faith that embraced Christ as Saviour, as the Acts of the Apostles shows, immediately declared itself in baptism. The renewed soul, anxious as Saul of Tarsus to know what the Lord would have him do, will not stop to ask if the rite is essential to salvation. It is enough for him that the terms of the commission for the evangelization of the world call for the baptism of believers. The rite does not take away the filth of the flesh, but is the response of a good conscience towards God (1 Pet. 3:21).

The signs following (vv. 17-18) are the credentials of the faith. In their literal aspect they were the authenticating marks of the new movement. The miracles of Moses before Pharaoh authenticated his mission. The miracles of our Lord were a part of the proof of His Messiahship. The early signs and wonders of the Acts were the necessary accompaniment of the new movement of Christianity, and were to cease when it was established. We see most of these signs fulfilled in the early ministry of Peter and of Paul. Truly the Jews who sought after signs had them given for a time, both in the ministry of the Servant on earth and the work He carried on from heaven. We read that the great salvation which began to be spoken by the Lord was confirmed to us by them that heard Him, God bearing witness by signs and wonders and gifts of the Holy Ghost-according to His own will (Heb. 2:4). These are the signs of Mark 16.

The death of Jesus discounted His signs and wonders, the Jews would affirm. Were there any new signs and wonders to authenticate the preaching of His resurrection? The Spirit of God answers in the affirmative, and indicates them in the Acts of the Apostles. As ever, these are withdrawn as soon as the new movement is established. They evidently ceased during the lifetime of Paul. When he left Trophimus at Miletum sick (2 Tim. 4:20), and told Timothy to drink no longer water but use a little wine for his stomach's sake and his often infirmities (1 Tim. 5:23), he had not lost his power with God. These sign gifts had ceased as would the tongues (1 Cor. 13:8).

The spiritual counterpart of these signs would go on. In the symbolic and greater sense they would continue in the world. Miracles in the realm of spirit, soul, and body would accompany the faith wherever preached. Satan in devilish dispositions and destructive influences would be driven out of men and of nations, and health of soul and body be the result of faith in Christ. Upon the believers themselves the signs of changed tongues, miraculous deliverances, and of restored health would be seen. These were the greater works that the disciples would do when Jesus was glorified (Jn. 14:12).

The attempts in these days to demonstrate a literal fulfillment of these signs are pathetic and foolish, as a rule. Men and women who obviously have a superficial grasp of the Word of God and consequently of sin, "speak with tongues," claim amazing miracles of healing, and are

seen juggling with snakes, all the while drawing attention to themselves and not to Christ, who ever is
supreme when the Holy Spirit acts in men. None of us
may state with certainty what God never does; but the
normal procedure of spiritual movements today will look
for Him to grant signs which correspond symbolically
with those indicated by our Lord here.

Mark takes our Lord to the throne of God, continuing
the work He had begun below. What a tireless worker He
is, and how it encourages our hearts to know that He
works with us, confirming the Word with signs following.

It is suggestive to note the charter of the missionary
church as seen at the end of each of the four Gospels.
Matthew, once in an official position himself, writes of
the King coming to Israel. In resurrection, He commands His servants to make disciples of all nations. He
is left on earth, for He must reign. Mark, as we have
seen, failed at first as a missionary, but he came back to
win the commendation of aged Paul. There is a brevity, a
breathlessness, about the Gospel of Mark that is arrest-
ing, as he tells of the diligence and devotion of the
Perfect Servant. He takes Christ to heaven and assures
the missionary that He still works from heaven with him.
Luke is the sympathetic man, a beloved physician, who
writes of the Son of Man. Recognizing the frailties of the
missionary, he bids him tarry until he is endued with
power from on high.

Thus the Spirit is introduced into the great commission, the power for service. The ascended Lord leaves

the disciples worshiping and praising God in the temple, for the missionary must not only be a worker but a worshiper. Constant service will soon leave him weary and often disappointed. The missionary must, above all things, maintain his link with God in worship and praise. This gives freshness to his ministry and joy to his soul. He who waits for power, and praises while he waits, will do better work for God than he who thinks it is spiritual to always be on the go.

John would remind the missionary of his delegated authority. *"As My Father hath sent Me, even so send I you"* (Jn. 20:21). We can only go forth in His Name as we, too, go out from the bosom of the Father. The authority is not our own. Luke tells us that Jesus showed His disciples His hands and His feet; John says He showed them His hands and His side. The wounds of Christ impart not only peace to the heart and power to the hands, but wings to the feet of the evangelist.

Thus he has the command of the King, the cooperation of the Servant, power by the Spirit, and divine authority in his message. Father, Son, and Spirit are with him in the glorious evangel.

Our Lord's last recorded words in the Gospels are not about His glorious return, but of the program and provision of the great commission is to evangelize the world. Surely we cannot do better than have it before us always. He would not have us *"stand gazing up to heaven,"* but witnessing for Him in Jerusalem and Judea, in Samaria, and to the uttermost part of the earth.

EIGHT

The Life After Death

*But now is Christ risen from the dead, and becomes the
firstfruits of them that slept...But every man in his own
order: Christ the firstfruits; afterward they
that are Christ's at His coming.*
1 CORINTHIANS 15:20, 23

The first Epistle of Paul to the Corinthians has much
to say about the gathering, gifts, and government of the
local church. For this reason, in these days when every
man does that which is right in his own eyes in things
ecclesiastical, the book is often neglected. Rightly
understood, it deals a death blow to much that passes for
the mind of God in matters concerning the Church.
There is much to correct in the letter because of the local
aspect of it, but principles are furnished for us in similar
circumstances today. Christ crucified is emphasized at

the beginning, Christ raised from the dead at the end. Christ crucified, foolish in the eyes of the world, is found to be the very wisdom of God, and by which people are saved (1 Cor. 1:18). Christ raised—denied by some—is found to be abundantly proved and to be the pattern of the resurrection of His people. Their life after death is assured in His.

The preaching of resurrection (1 Cor. 15:1-4):

For I delivered unto you first of all that which I also received, how that Christ died for our sins according to the Scriptures; and that He was buried, and that He rose again the third day according to the Scriptures.

The apostle is careful to tell us throughout the book that he is but a steward of his doctrine, declaring what he had received from the Lord. Even after showing the liberty of two or three to speak in the church and of the silence of women in that ministry, he insists that the spiritual will acknowledge that these are the commands of the Lord (see 1 Cor. 14:29-37). In chapter 15, the gospel he had received consisted in Christ dying, according to the Scriptures; Christ buried; and Christ rising again, according to the Scriptures. The resurrection was fundamental to the preaching of both Paul and Peter. Christ's death was not only at the hands of men, but at the hands of God. It was for our sins, according to Isaiah 53.

But the world had no proof of the fullness and finality of His atonement, apart from His rising. He who was *"delivered for our offenses...was raised again for our justification"* (Rom. 4:25). Having *"purged our sins, [He] sat down on the right hand of the Majesty on high"* (Heb. 1:3). This was the message that turned the world upside down, and still does when preached in the energy of the Spirit of God.

The proof of resurrection (vv. 5-11): Sevenfold proof is given here of Christ's being seen alive after His passion. The Scriptures are first. The resurrection is anticipated clearly in Psalm 22 and in Isaiah 53, where the suffering One, after His piercing and being brought into death, sings in the midst of the Church. Psalm 102 is a conversation between the Father and the Son, as Hebrews 1:8-12 clearly shows.

> *But Thou, O Lord, shalt endure for ever; and Thy remembrance unto all generations. Thou shalt arise, and have mercy upon Zion...Of old hast Thou laid the foundations of the earth: and the heavens are the work of Thy hands. They shall perish, but Thou shalt endure.*

The Scriptures thus lead us to expect not only a suffering Messiah, but a resurrected one.

Second, *"He was seen of Cephas."* Our Lord's grace to one who denied Him is indicated here. *"Go your way, tell His disciples and Peter,"* are words recorded only by Mark, who was acutely aware of his own defection. *"The Lord is risen indeed, and hath appeared unto Simon,"* writes Luke. What grace! Surely my denial can never quench His love, nor sever His relations with me. *"And Peter... ";* how many have taken courage from the words, and dared to believe that though they had believed not, yet He would always abide faithful. We shall, like Peter, weep over our failure, but we shall be encouraged by these words to creep back to the shelter of His forgiving arms.

Third, *"then of the twelve."* Judas Iscariot had been one of the twelve, but had not witnessed the resurrection. He was dead, and Matthias had replaced him, being one who had been a witness of the things concerning Christ from the baptism of John until our Lord was taken up to heaven (Acts 1:22, 26). The administrative number was thus complete.

Fourth, *"after that, He was seen of above five hundred brethren at once; of whom the greater part remain unto this present, but some are fallen asleep"* (1 Cor. 15:6). This large number, of whom Paul could assert that the majority were living witnesses, precludes, as we have said before, the idea of either fraud or hallucination. This was doubtless the gathering by appointment in Galilee. The fraud theory would assert that the disciples were dishonest men who knew that Jesus was dead and went to corruption, but preached His rising from the dead. Thus we would have the anomaly of men dying in terrible torments for a fraud, and making the world virtuous through lies. Men work fraud for base gain. Whoever heard of men putting over a fraud for the sole reward of dying in torment! These witnesses lost everything, judged by earthly standards, for their testimony—friends, fortune, life itself. Under the most excruciating pain, these witnesses gave the costly evidence of their veracity, never breaking down and confessing fraud. Their voluntary martyrdom is evidence of their truthfulness. Otherwise, under pressure of the sword and the flame and the lions in the arena, some of them would have recanted.

The witnesses were too many to deceive. It is significant that none of the opponents of Christianity accused these witnesses of fraud. Show us men who, without personal gain, will die in horrible torments for what they affirm, and we will show you men who give the highest evidence of their veracity.

So also with hallucination. While one or two might conceivably have been deceived in the early light of the morning, above five hundred at one time scarcely could be. These men were mightily convinced and prepared to die for their convictions. They could not have had the body of Jesus hidden away while dying for a faith that proclaimed His rising. And the enemies of Jesus only had to produce His body to put an end to the new movement. If friend or foe could not produce it, He must have risen as He said.

The more modern myth theory—that it was only with the passing of years that the doctrine of a resurrected Jesus was promulgated—is equally untenable, in the light of the graves of the martyrs in the catacombs at Rome. There we see the early inscriptions to a living faith in the resurrection from earliest times.

Fifth, *"after that, He was seen of James."* This is probably the Lord's brother and the author of the epistle that bears his name. The personal appearance to James is not recorded but evidently well known. It had been recorded that *"neither did His brethren believe in Him"* (Jn. 7:5), but now James, at least, is out in the light, and a representative of those who had come into faith by the culminating fact of resurrection.

Sixth, *"then of all the apostles."* This was doubtless the larger number of those who saw His ascension from the Mount of Olives (Lk. 24:50). They really saw Him go and were assured by the angels that this same Jesus would return in like manner.

Seventh, *"last of all, He was seen of me also, as of one born out of due time."* Paul's vision on the Damascus road was not a phantom-like appearance of the Saviour. Paul is prepared to make it a mark of his apostleship. *"Am I not an apostle?...have I not seen Jesus Christ our Lord?"* (1 Cor. 9:1). It was *"the Lord...that appeared unto [him] in the way,"* and Paul would, like the others, die for his faith. He seems to regard his rebirth in Christ as premature—*"out of due time"*—an anticipation of the time when a nation will look to Him whom they pierced, and be born. Paul was given a sight of the risen Christ with his eyes, and regarded himself as the prototype of his people after the flesh, who shall see and believe.

The great change wrought in the erstwhile persecutor of the church is a potent argument for Christianity. The change in the day, from the seventh to the first day of the week; the change in the disciples, from fear and defeat to courage and victory; and the change in the destroyer of the church is a threefold cord of proof not quickly broken. *"Benjamin shall ravin as a wolf: in the morning he shall devour the prey, and at night he shall divide the spoil"* (Gen. 49:27). So wrote Jacob of his son Benjamin. *"Breathing out threatenings and slaughter against the disciples of the Lord"* (Acts 9:1), devouring the prey indeed, Paul was converted to the cause he was persecuting, and in the evening of his life he shared the spoils of his victories for Christ.

The pledge of resurrection (vv. 12-34):

But now is Christ risen from the dead, and become the firstfruits of them that slept. For since by man came death, by man came also the resurrection of the dead. For as in Adam all die, even so in Christ shall all be made alive. But every man in his own order: Christ the firstfruits; afterward they that are Christ's at His coming.

Seven calamities are indicated if the doctrine of the resurrection be denied. It appears that it was not simply the resurrection of Jesus that was denied by some, but resurrection itself. The inspired apostle meets this Gentile Sadduceeism (Mk. 12:18), after his sevenfold positive witness of resurrection, by an equally strong negative one. Sometimes a doctrine of Scripture is emphasized if we consider what is involved in a denial of it. The truth of the virgin birth of our Lord is one of these. We must discount the testimony of the angel Gabriel, of Mary the mother of Joseph, of Elizabeth, of Simeon and Anna, and of Luke a beloved physician, the last who states his thorough knowledge of all things from the very first (Lk. 1:3), if we deny the divine entrance into the world of that divine Person. A denial stains the very character of God, blackens the fair name of Mary, degrades Christ to the human level, impeaches the testimony of Zacharias, Elizabeth, Simeon, and Anna, and denies the statements of Luke the historian. Yet these witnesses are of good character. Their evidence is credible. Greater difficulties are created by the denial of the doctrine than by its acceptance. So also here.

1. *"If there be no resurrection of the dead, then is Christ not risen"* (v. 13). A denial of the resurrection, *per se*, sets aside with a wave of the hand all the testimony of Scripture and of Jesus Himself, who as plainly declared His rising again as His approaching death. Under this assumption that there is no resurrection, Jesus is plainly dead.

2. *"Our preaching is vain"* (v. 14). All the expenditure of preaching Jesus and the resurrection, in those costly days of the propagation of Christianity, was to no purpose. The baptism of water—and of blood—of those early confessors of the Christ, was a vain thing. It was for the dead they were baptized, if the dead rose not. This is probably the force of the much disputed verse 29. The word *"dead"* is in the plural and can hardly refer to the dead Christ alone. The apostle seems to say, "Else what shall they do who are baptized? It is for the dead, if the dead rise not at all. Why then be baptized for dead persons?" There was no point to stepping into the thinning ranks of the soldiers of Christ, no point in seeking

to propagate a "dead" faith. The mighty efforts to preach the gospel to every creature is a useless dissipation of time and energy. Let us put an end to the building of churches and to the sending forth of missionaries at home and abroad. Let us stop the waste of highly trained workers and expensive equipment, in the preaching of a dead Christ. He is gone forever, and we cannot even point with certainty to His tomb.

3. *"Your faith is also vain"* (v. 14). The Corinthians and all others who have embraced the Christian faith are deceived. They have put good faith in a bad thing. Like honest people who have placed their hard-earned money in a bad bank and lost it all, those who have invested faith and labor and sacrifice in the Christian message have lost their souls and wasted their substance. They have leaned upon a staff and it has failed them; upon a reed and it has pierced their hand (Isa. 36:6). Faith is vain.

4. *"We are found false witnesses of God"* (v. 15). The testimony of the disciples of Jesus and of the Apostle Paul, as we have indicated, is impeached if we deny the truth of life after death.

5. *"Ye are yet in your sins"* (v. 17). There is no such experience as being "born again," or "saved," or "knowing that you have passed from death unto life." Any change that might appear to be wrought is not spiritual but psychological. There is no saving virtue in having

faith in a dead Jesus, any more than in a dead Mohammed or a dead Confucius. Yet millions of people all down the centuries have rejoiced in the knowledge of salvation, they claim. They have heard the gospel, as defined in verses 3-4 of 1 Corinthians 15, and it has *"effectually worked in them that believe"* (1 Thess. 2:13). Like these Thessalonians, they have turned to God from idols, to serve the living and true God. They have found that the knowledge of the living Christ has armed their nerves for fight against evil, has succored them in temptation, has comforted them in sickness and bereavement, and pillowed their heads in death. But the deniers of resurrection today would treat the testimony of nineteen centuries as a fabrication. We are yet in our sins.

6. *"They also which are fallen asleep in Christ are perished"* (v. 18). The Corinthian saints would never again see their loved ones who had died in the faith if there were no resurrection. Nor would we. We would not see or meet our loved ones again. Absent from the body, they are not with the Lord. We can only, at best, stand at the grave of our departed and, with Colonel Robert Ingersol say:

> *Is there beyond the silent grave*
> *An endless day?*
> *Is death a gate that leads to life?*
> *We cannot say.*
> *The tongueless secret locked in fate*
> *We do not know:*
> *We hope...we wait.*

7. *"We are of all men most miserable"* (v. 19). If non-resurrection makes the fate of our faithful dead unknown, our own state is otherwise. *"Most miserable"* describes us. If hope deferred makes the heart sick, we are in a worse state, for we have no hope at all. We cannot stand and say, *"O death, where is thy sting? O grave, where is thy victory?"* (1 Cor. 15:55). We are bereft and beaten, and can but look forward to the dread prospect of our own hopeless departure.

Great calamities indeed! No reason for faith, no redemption for the fallen, no reunion of friends, no rejoicing in the future. All, all is lost, if there be no resurrection.

"But now is Christ risen from the dead, and become the firstfruits of them that slept" (v. 20). The triumphant cry of the apostle breaks forth amid the gloom. In Christ shall all be made alive. He is the firstfruits; afterward they that are His at His coming. The apostle here is not speaking of the effects of the resurrection as they appear to the world at large, but to those *"that are Christ's."* God has

> *...appointed a day, in the which He will judge the world in righteousness by that man whom He hath ordained; whereof He hath given assurance unto all men, in that He hath raised Him from the dead* (Acts 17:31).

> *The hour is coming, in the which all that are in the graves shall hear His voice, and shall come forth; they that have*

*done good, unto the resurrection of life; and they that have
done evil, unto the resurrection of judgment* (Jn. 5:28-29).

Righteous retribution is thus pledged by God to a
guilty world by the rising again of Christ. Here, however,
the welcome change from corruption to incorruption,
from dishonor to glory, from weakness to power, from a
natural to a spiritual body, is pledged to those who,
believing the gospel delivered to them, have thus not
believed in vain. Christ raised is the promise of a harvest
to come. He is the Forerunner, who for us has entered
heaven (Heb. 6:20). He is the Corn of Wheat which fell
into the ground and died, but which brings forth much
fruit.

In the rain forest in Olympic National Park in the state
of Washington we saw rows of stately trees and giant
ferns growing out of the decayed length of giant firs.
The soft, moist heart of the old log furnished the ideal
conditions for the young seeds to grow. Out of death had
come life, vigorous and beautiful.

The Lord is risen indeed. Then there *is* reason for
faith, and preaching *is not* in vain. There is redemption
for fallen humanity: we are not yet in our sins. We shall
see again our loved ones who have died in Christ, for
there will be a great reunion above. We shall be caught
up together with them, to meet the Lord in the air. We
are not of all men most miserable. We fearlessly face the
future and joyfully anticipate the day of His coming. The
firstfruits has been raised—afterward shall all who are
His. What a pledge we have in the glory of His rising!

4. The pattern of resurrection (vv. 35-50):

But some man will say, How are the dead raised up? and with what body do they come? Thou fool, that which thou sowest is not quickened, except it die: and that which thou sowest, thou sowest not that body that shall be, but bare grain, it may chance of wheat, or of some other grain: but God giveth it a body as it hath pleased Him, and to every seed his own body. all flesh is not the same flesh...One star differeth from another star in glory. So also is the resurrection of the dead...As we have borne the image of the earthy, we shall also bear the image of the heavenly.

That the Apostle Paul does not deem the questions, as propounded in verse 35, foolish seems clear from the verses which follow, in which he seeks to answer them in part. It is rather the derisive unbelief that would suppose the questions incapable of an answer, that Paul attacks. They are like the questions of the Sadducees concerning a resurrection in which they did not believe. The apostle decries the caviling, but considers the questions worth facing. Not that he considers them worthy of an apologetic, of which the apostle is so able when necessity arises, as the books of Romans and Galatians show. But he is not anxious to be explicit where the Scripture or the Spirit of God is reticent. Both Paul and John knew that *"it doth not yet appear what we shall be"* (1 Jn. 3:2).

But nature provided an analogy and, in part, a solution to the questions which Paul anticipates will be asked about the resurrection body. The seed in the ground and the stars in the sky will be enough to suggest a pattern of resurrection. There is evident relation between that which goes into the ground and that which is the result of the dying of the seed. Only that which was, can be raised, and that which sleeps, be awakened. There is no force in the term "resurrection" if no definite relation and identification with the old identity is preserved. *"Thou sowest not that body that shall be"* (1 Cor. 15:37). If wheat is sown, wheat is raised, but not the particular grains originally put in the earth.

We need not speculate on the continuance of matter in the body that goes into the grave, and its association in the body that shall be. God gives a body as it pleases Him, but is pleased to tell us that there will be identity, an association between that which is sown and that which shall be raised. The use of the word *"it"* in verses 41-42 demands this. The human body maintains its resemblance and personality throughout its earthly life, although its component parts are changed each seven years, and the body is in a state of constant flux. It is ever replacing that which has become waste and effete. The body of the man is not, as to its matter, the body of the child from which it was developed. Yet identification is possible. We recognize the man from the picture of the child. That identification did not depend on the preservation of the same identical particles that compose it.

So also in the resurrection. Though no particles might remain of that original body which clothes the human spirit, God will give that renewed spirit a body as it pleases Him, and which will bear such substance, similarity and identity as to cause us to say with our Lord in

His rising, *"Handle Me and see that it is I Myself."*

Here the analogy seems to cease, for, while in nature the seed bears an abundance, it may be, of seeds like itself, the spiritual sowing of one body, as to the believer, results in the raising of one body in surpassing and fadeless beauty. Our Lord was the corn of wheat which fell into the ground and died, and in dying brought forth much fruit; but our glorified body will be the result of that individual sowing, of that death in the Lord.

"With what body do they come?" (1 Cor. 15:35). It is sown in corruption, but raised in incorruption. It is sown in dishonor, but raised in glory. It is sown in weakness, but raised in power. It is sown a natural body, but raised a spiritual body. We shall come in an incorruptible, glorified, powerful, spiritual body. If ours is to be made like His glorious body (Phil. 3:21), it may be like the body of our Lord in resurrection—of flesh and bones. In verse 50 we are told that *"flesh and blood cannot inherit the kingdom of God"* (meaning those who are alive in their present bodies); *"neither doth corruption inherit incorruption"* (meaning those who have died in that body). The function of the blood is to convey to the tissues, ever decaying and dying, the elements supplied by food for their continual repair. No such function will be necessary in the house from heaven.

The resurrection body will be different from the old, a heavenly body fitted for a new environment. It will be *"a building of God, an house not made with hands"* (2 Cor. 5:1). As we have borne the image of the earthy, recognizing and being recognized one of another, so shall we bear the image of the heavenly, and know even as also we are known.

Paul's illustration of the stars would lead us also to believe that there will be differences in glory in the new bodies. We shall not be exact replicas of one another. *"One star differeth from another star in glory. So also in the resurrection of the dead"* (1 Cor. 15:41). A Paul who finished his course with joy may shine brighter than a Demas who forsook him, having loved this present world. *"They that be wise shall shine as the brightness of the firmament; and they that turn many to righteousness as the stars for ever and ever"* (Dan. 12:3).

To this may be added that our new bodies shall not need an organism for the fresh supply of that which is wasting away, since there will no longer be any decay. Nor will the relations necessary for the reproduction of the race continue, since there will be no more death. We shall stand complete in eternal life.

Putting all these things together, we see something of the pattern of that life after death, serving our Lord in a body incorruptible, glorious, powerful, heavenly, and eternal. For this we wait, sometimes groaning in this present tabernacle, for the consummation of our adoption, the redemption of the body. Then it shall be manifest what we are, the sons of God (Rom. 8:19). We shall be bearing the image of the heavenly. We shall be like Him morally. We shall see Him as He is.

5. The Period of Resurrection (vv. 51-58).

Behold, I show you a mystery; we shall not all sleep, but

*we shall all be changed, in a moment, in the twinkling of
an eye, at the last trump: for the trumpet shall sound, and
the dead shall be raised incorruptible, and we shall be
changed. For this corruptible must put on incorruption,
and this mortal must put on immortality.*

The mystery, the thing not revealed until this point,
was not that they should not all sleep. Paul had made this
known in a letter to the Thessalonians some five years
before. But he had not indicated then that there would be
any change in that which would be raised. It took this
later communication to show that there would be, and a
later revelation still to show that nothing less than glorious likeness to Christ is the future transfiguration for
these present bodies of ours (Phil. 3:21).

"We shall not all sleep." Writing to the Thessalonians,
Paul stated, *"If we believe that Jesus died and rose
again, even so them also which sleep in Jesus will God
bring with Him"* (1 Thess. 4:14). It was death for Jesus;
it is sleep for us. It would have been death for us, the
first and second death, had He not died and brought life
and immortality to light through the gospel. For us to die
is but to sleep, for there is the certainty of awakening in
the morning. We rest from our labors, and rise to serve
again in newness of life and body.

The period is *"at the last trump...at His coming"* (vv.
52, 23). The last trump may be another of the metaphors
which the apostle often borrows from Roman military
life. The protection of the garrison, the posting of the
sentinel, the triumph of the victorious army, are all used

by Paul to assure and charge the people. Here it seems to refer to the trumpet calls to arouse sleeping soldiers, to strike tents and get ready to move, and the last trump to march away. Trumpets were used in the calling of the assembly of Israel, and for special and sudden directions to a people spread far apart because of their numbers; but it would seem, as is usual with Paul, that the illustration is from Roman and not Jewish life. The trumpet shall arouse the sleeping saints, even the trump of God (1 Thess. 4:16). No interval need be given then to prepare for the journey, for the change will take place in a moment, in the twinkling of an eye. How gladly will we be done with the present tent, for we that are in this tabernacle do groan. What joy to be clothed upon with our house from heaven. The new body will not be a tent, symbol of our earthly sojourn, but a house in which we shall dwell forever.

His rising insures all this for us. *"Because I live, ye shall live also"* (Jn. 14:19). Life after death is as certain for us as for Him. *"Christ the firstfruits; afterward they that are Christ's at His coming"* (1 Cor. 15:23). And the signs are not wanting that this "afterward" is about to become a reality in our lives.

> *Blessed be the God and Father of our Lord Jesus Christ, which according to His abundant mercy hath begotten us again unto a lively hope by the resurrection of Jesus Christ from the dead, To an inheritance incorruptible, and undefiled, and that fadeth not away, reserved in heaven for you, Who are kept by the power of God...* (1 Pet. 1:3-5).